THE *first* AUSTRALIAN DICTIONARY OF VULGARITIES & OBSCENITIES

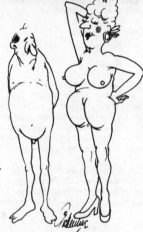

Text:
BOB HUDSON
Illustration:
LARRY PICKERING

David & Charles
Newton Abbot   London

FOREWORD

British Library Cataloguing in Publication Data

Hudson, Bob
  The first Australian dictionary of
  vulgarities & obscenities.
  I. Title   II. Pickering, Larry
  828   PR9619.3.H8/

  ISBN 0-7153-9054-6

First published in 1986
by Lilyfield Publishers Pty Ltd
2 Aquatic Drive, French's Forest
NSW 2086. Australia

First published in Great Britain in 1987
by David & Charles Publishers plc

© Lilyfield Publishers.
© Bob Hudson, Larry Pickering.

Concept: Nicholas Brash

Printed in Great Britain
by Billings & Sons Ltd, Worcester
for David & Charles Publishers plc
Brunel House   Newton Abbot   Devon

RS = rhyming slang
rcs = {racial / ethnic} -slur (though not always a slur)

FOREWORD FOR LEXICOGRAPHERS

Vulgar and obscene expressions from around the world have become part of the Australian language. Words without an obvious historical link with Australia, recent imports via TV and movies for example, were tested rigorously as per Rule 3 of the Junior Lexicographers' Handbook: we used them in the pub and if someone threatened to job us, into the book they went.

FOREWORD FOR NICE, DECENT, REFINED PERSONS

Please do not believe anything you have read thus far. Pickering and I were kidnapped and forced at gunpoint to produce this book. We are deeply, deeply ashamed.

Afghan's fly trap

A. The big A (giving someone): to give them the arse, to eject them, to terminate a relationship. (ω)

Abo. Aboriginal (abbrev.) res

Abo's armpit. Unit of measurement of uncleanliness.

Ac-dc. Bi-sexual bi ὁμοϕ

Ace. The anus. The cheerful greeting ω ι of 'G'day Ace' can be given a second level of meaning by those in the know.

Acid. To put the acid on: to demand information or money.

• **Acre.** The buttocks. The novel *God's* ω *Little Acre* caused much unintentional mirth in the Antipodes.

Afghan's fly trap. Hole cut in one's trousers to draw flies from the face.

Afterbirth. Rhubarb (army slang).

After dinner mint. Sex in exchange ϕ for dinner.

Agates. Testicles. A connie agate was a favourite type of marble years ago — when marbles were really made of marble, not glass.

Alec. A con man's victim. Hence a Smart Alec — someone too clever to be conned.

Alec the phallic. Affectionate name for the penis.

Alive and kicking. Very much alive.

Alkie. Alcoholic, a deadbeat.

All alone like a country dunny. Isolated. *'toilet'*

All laired-up. Dressed to kill.

All piss 'n' wind. Full of folly and delusion (see bullshit). One can be 'all full of piss and wind like a barber's cat' who eats shaving lather thinking it is cream.

Amber fluid. Beer. A fond euphemism used by all manner of disgusting pisspots.

Animal act. Low act, despicable. A group of men may decide to have an animal night, perhaps a bucks' night, where it is understood that the normal conventions of civilised behaviour will be waived.

Ankle biter. An infant, toddler. American equivalent is rug-rat.

Ants (in your pants). Edgy, irritable, nervous.

Antsy. on the lookout for a sexual partner.

Any. (are you getting any?). Sexual intercourse. A young journalist once shyly asked Germaine Greer about her social life during a visit home to Australia. 'You mean am I getting any,' she replied. 'I have a lot of old friends here, they wouldn't see me go short.'

Apeshit. Wildly enthusiastic. "The crowd just went apeshit when the band came on stage."

Apples. She's apples. Okay. Everything's ok. Also breasts, as in a nice pair of apples.

Arab. A foreigner. Can also describe wild youths. Someone who fails to shut a door may be asked 'Were you born in a tent?' If the cheeky reply is 'Yes' it can be topped with: 'Well, shut the bloody flap.'

• **Argus Tuft.** Popular name for a racehorse, boat etc. The idea is to trick the authorities into allowing 'ah, get stuffed' as an official name (and to amuse passers-by).

Aristotle. Bottle (rhyming slang from Cockney).

Arse. The anus. Also: A despised person. Also: Good luck.
  (1) Arse about (face). In illogical order.
  (2) Arse over tit. Fall heavily or

upside down.

(3) Arse about. To fool around.

(4) Arse up. To bungle.

(5) The arse (give someone the arse). To sack.

(6) Arse into gear. To get going.

(7) Kiss my arse. Piss off! (see Piss).

(8) Arse from his elbow (wouldn't know). To distinguish clearly (also in neg. form).

(9) Pain in the arse. A bore. A nuisance.

(10) Smart arse. A know-all.

• (11) The sun shines out of his arse. He can't do a thing wrong.

(12) More arse than class. Succeeding by luck and boldness.

Arse bandit. An aggressive homosexual. (see Transmitter).

Arsehole. The anus. Also a despised place. (this is the arsehole of the earth).

To eject someone, kick them out. Can be literal, to arsehole someone from the bar or figurative; "Janelle arseholed me the other night" (meaning the course of true love has run out). A strong derogatory term (unlike bastard or bugger), arsehole is not a term one would normally use when chiacking friends. Also:

• (1) As ugly as a bag full of arseholes. Really ugly! Alternatively, a face like a hatful of monkeys' arseholes.

(2) From arsehole to breakfast. Completely or totally. (He kicked

him from arsehole to breakfast).
· (3) As long as your arsehole points to the ground. While you're still standing.

Arse-licker. A crawler or sycophant.

Arsy. Dead lucky. (Gawd, he's arsy!)

Artichoke. A decrepit retired prostitute.

Artist. An expert. Bull artist. Panic artist. Booze artist.

Arty-farty. Pseudo. Pretentious.Also artsy-fartsy. Applies as much to the new wave of community artists who insist on covering public walls with socially redeeming murals as it does to the tuxedo and opening night set.

Aspro. A male prostitute.

Aunty. The ABC, or Australian Broadcasting Corporation. First to deliberately broadcast the magic word (Fuck) though the organisation does have other claims to fame.

Aunt Mary. The toilet. Gone to visit Aunt Mary is a polite way of saying gone to the dunny.

Aunt Nellie. Belly.

Auntie's downfall: Gin. (As in mother's ruin).

Australian salute. The movement of brushing bush flies away from the face.

Axe. To sack or dismiss an employee.

Also 'having an axe to grind'. Having an ulterior motive.

(ω) **Axe handle.** Unit of measurement, usually of buttock width. 'She was three axe handles wide'.

Beaver

B

B. Euphemistic abbrev. Bastard. (He's a right B). Often confused with that other old Australian term of abuse, bugger. (See SOB).

Babe. A girl or sweetheart. (♀)

B and D. Bondage and Disciple. Prostitute argot for sado-masochistic (⊗) sex. Also a well-known brand of garage door, so be specific when ordering.

Back. Back up for more. To come back for seconds.

Backfire. To break wind.

Backside. The part up which tardy or lazy people are kicked.

Back door. The anus.

Back door merchant. A homosexual. ὅμοφ ♂

Back garden. The anus.

Back hander.
(1) A bribe, often to police.

(2) A casual blow popular with wife beaters and child abusers.

Back of beyond. phr. An impossibly remote place.

Back way. The anus. One popular homosexual meeting place in Sydney has closed off the main street foyer with a sign reading: Entrance at Rear.

Bacon. Bring home the bacon, to succeed. To win money at the races.

Bad egg. A no-hoper. A villain.

Bad lot. A villain, no-hoper.

Bad news. A person you don't want to meet. 'Dodge Jack, he's bad news.'

Bag. To condemn or criticise. Also an unattractive woman.

Bag of rats. Mess, confusion.

Bag of shit. A person of whom one has a bad opinion.

Bag of wind. A bore. Non-stop talker. (See Politician).

Bagging. Severe criticism.(See Politician).

Bag man. Holder of illicit money. (See Politician).

Bali belly. Diarrhoea. Be warned by a Sydney journalist who beshat himself on the foyer of the Sanur Beach Hotel and said in excuse: 'I thought I'd only farted.'. The Americans call it Montezuma's Revenge (they blame the

nearest offshore holiday venue just as
we do).

Ball and chain. The wife. On a
buck's night a man about to be
married may be carted around town
wearing a ball and chain in dual
celebration of his heritage and his
future.

(♀)

Ballarat Jewshop. A messy, untidy
place.

Balls. Testicles.
(1) Balls and all. Wholeheartedly.
(2) Do one's balls. Fall madly in love.
(3) Balls-up. A blunder. (See
    Politician).
(4) By the balls. (Have someone by). In
    your power.
(5) He's got balls! (Courage).
(6) Balls around. To fool about.

∞

*Also cock-up.

φ ?

Ball-tearer. Ripper! Terrific. Used to
describe the breaking of anything
from Olympic records to wind. Cod
Ripper is a more coy version.

(ω)

Balt. Baltic migrant after World War
II (included Poles and Hungarians!)

res

Band. A prostitute.

(♀) ⊗

Bandicoot. Small Australian
marsupial corrupted as in
(1) Bald as a bandicoot. Completely
    bald.
(2) Barmy as . . . mad
(3) Poor as . . . wretchedly poor.

φ ρ er

Band moll. Young girl who has sex

(♀) $

with rock groups. (See groupie). No word exists yet for young women who have sex with rock group roadies or managers. Australian vulgarity will not have come fully into flower until this breach is filled. Pig and scumsucker have already been rejected as inadequate.

Bang. To have sex. A woman is said to bang, though for some reason a man does not. Nor does a couple bang, though they may root.
(1) Bang like a shithouse door in a gale.
(2) Bang like a dunny door in the wind (see Go off).
A bang was also an early term for a brothel.

Bar. I won't have a bar of it. To not tolerate something.

Barbie. Barbecue. Also three or four snags short of a barbie: stupid. Also an expensive children's toy with realistic breasts but not the other bits.

Barebum. A short (often military style) dinner jacket.

Bark. To vomit. (see Yawn).

Barmaid's blush. A drink of rum and raspberry or port and lemonade. Any drink designed to disguise the flavour or presence of alcohol. (See Leg opener).

Barmy. Mad, silly.

Barney. A fight, usually without dire

results. The protagonists will speak lightly of 'having a bit of a barney'.

Barrel. To knock down. (Esp at football . . . he was barreled). Also: Your turn in the barrel. A suggestion may be made to a member of an all-male gathering that the only way anyone will get any sex is for a volunteer to provide it from the anonymity of a barrel. This saying is based on several old jokes and folk tales but rarely put into effect because of a shortage of barrels.

Barrenjoey. A prostitute. ☿

Barrow. To push or back up one's barrow.

Bart. A girl of loose character. A 'nice' way of saying tart used by bush balladists last century. RS (♀)

Base. Buttocks. Also base over apex. To fall or tumble. (See Arse over tit). ω

Bash. A party.

Bash. To talk incessantly. To ear-bash. Also to physically assault. In the great Australian tradition of recreational violence bashings are usually performed on schoolmates or drinking companions, generally the smallest or drunkest respectively. An altercation between two people of equal pugilistic skill is not a bashing but a fight and not nearly as much fun.

Basket. Euphemism for bastard.

Bastard. An unpleasant person. Originally, a person of unconventional ancestry. Also

(1) A right bastard of a day. A rotten day.

• (2) Happy as a bastard on Father's Day. Morose.

(3) Don't let the bastards grind you down. Keep cheerful.

Bastardise. To corrupt or mangle. Also a popular form of bullying initiation in military academies or private schools. These institutions issue annual denials that such things happen, which makes you wonder doesn't it?

Bat. An ugly or objectionable (old) woman.
Also:

(1) Blind as a bat. Very short-sighted.

(2) (Like a) bat out of hell. At full speed.

(3) Bat and bowl. Bi-sexual. 'He/she bats and bowls'.

Bathouse. A brothel.

Battleaxe. A domineering woman. The older models run the CWA, the younger ones run for public office as Democrats.

Battler. One who gets by on a limited income. This term implies great approval for the 'Little Aussie Battler' but was used last century to describe a prostitute.

Batty. Crazy.

Beam. Buttocks. Usually broad in the beam meaning big-arsed (see Arse).

Bear (with a sore head). Hungover.

Beat the meat. To masturbate.

Beat-up. An exaggerated newspaper story. See the front page of today's afternoon newspaper for an example.

Beaut. Fine! Great! Also you beaut.

Beaver. The vagina (US).

Bedourie (fly veil). Excrement on a shirt-tail designed to attract flies (cf Afhgan Fly Trap).

Bee.
(1) Bee in your bonnet. An obsession.
(2) Bee's knees. Something terrific. It's the bee's knees

Beef bayonet. An erect penis. (See Pork sword).

Beer gut. Abdominal evidence of a life of beer drinking. Debate continues to rage as to whether the beer gut should protrude over the trousers or be tucked under.

Beer mug. A chamber pot.

Bell. Phone call as in 'Give us a bell'.

Belly. Lower than a snake's belly. Despicable.

Bellybuster. A poor dive into water landing stomach first. (Also bellyflop).

Bellyful. A surplus intake as in 'a bellyful of beer'.

Bellygrunting. Indigestion. Guts ache.

ὄμοφ (♂)

Ben Doon. Apocryphal Scots sodomite. Friend of Philip McCavity.

Bend. Bend the elbow. Drink (beer) usually in excess.

Bender. A drinking spree.

folk etymology
(following uncon-
nected adaptation?)

Beresk. Corruption of berserk. Commonly misinterpreted to mean bereft or upset.

RS >

o >

• **Berk.** Cockney expression introduced via TV shows and enthusiastically adopted in Australia. From Berskhire Hunt: Cunt. Not descriptive of the female organs, used as term of abuse.

Bet. To wager, gamble.
(1) Bet London to a brick on. Odds-on.
(2) Bet Sydney to the bush. High-rolling betting.
(3) Bet your boots/life/arse on this. To bet on a certainty. Betcha. 'You betcha'. Certainly.

(♀)

Better half. One's wife or partner.

(φ)

• **B4 I $\sqrt{U}$ $\frac{RU}{16}$?** Mock scientific formula for sex. Transates as Before I Root You. Are You Over 16?

bi.

Bi. Abbrev for bi-sexual.

Bib and tucker. Best clothes.

✝

Bible-basher. A religious fanatic.

ω

Big A. The big Arse. Usually in dismissal. Getting the big A.

Big C. Cancer.

Big brown eyes. Breasts.

Big gun. A powerful person.

Big league. Big business/top strata. 'He's in the big league'.

Big-note. To boast. Also big-noter.

Big smoke. The city.

Big spit. Vomit.

ἐμετ.

Bike. A woman who sleeps with anyone. Also the town bike.

(♀)

Billy Muggins. A fool, the village idiot.

Bird.
(1) Make a bird of it. Succeed.
(2) To get the bird. To be booed off stage.
(3) Strictly for the birds. Trivial.
(4) Give someone the bird. To ridicule someone.
(5) A young woman. Anyone using this term is a dead giveaway Pom, or someone who has wasted years watching imported BBC comedy shows on TV.

< UK (♀)

Bird brain. A mental lightweight.

Bishop Barker. A tall beer glass named after the Anglican bishop of Sydney from 1845 to 1881 who was well over six feet tall.

Bit. Sexual intercourse.
(1) Did you get a bit last night?
(2) A bit on the side. Extra-marital sex.
(3) A bit each-way. Bi-sexual.

bi

Bite.
(1) Put the bite on someone. To borrow money.
(2) Bite the dust. To get knocked down.
(3) Bite an ear. To nag.

Bitser. A mongrel dog.

Bitumen blonde. Aboriginal woman.

Blackfellow's delight. Rum.

Black stump. A mythical milestone which marks some far horizon.
An official black stump now exists as a tourist attraction; it is about as authentic as the concrete Golden Triangle which has been built in the opium region of Northern Thailand.

Black velvet. Derog. term for an Aboriginal girl seen as a sex object.

Bladder. To have a Japanese/Woolworths bladder. To need to go the lavatory often.

Blakes. The Joe Blakes, rhyming slang, the shakes. Also a Joe Blake, a snake.

Blanks. To fire blanks, to be impotent.

Blind drunk. To be too drunk to see.

Blind Freddy. Someone incredibly obtuse. 'Even Blind Freddy can see that!'

Blind staggers. Extreme drunkenness.

Blinks. Cigarette ends. Collecting these to ensure a free supply of tobacco has become a lost art since the advent of the filter tip.

Blithered. Drunk.

Blob. A fat fool.

Block. To do one's block. To lose one's temper completely.

Blokery. Men, the masculine sphere.

Blood. Blood worth bottling. To describe a worthwhile person.

Bloodhole. The vagina.

Blonde. Media term for any woman not of Nubian ancestry involved in a sex crime, car accident or cheap publicity stunt. Stunning blonde: the same but with the added advantage of not being Quasimodo's sister.

Bloodhouse. An extremely rough hotel.

Blood oath. The universal Antipodean affirmative, a strong form of 'gosh yes'.

Bloody. To indicate approval. Bloody beauty, bloody good, bloody marvellous. Derived from an old oath (By Our Lady) bloody was used with glee by Protestants for centuries as an attack on Catholic loyalty to the Virgin Mary. Until quite recently it was considered a major swear word, due to the high proportion of Catholics (see Rockchoppers) in Australia, though most of the Catholics who found it offensive had long since forgotten the original meaning. Bloody is known as the great Australian adjective and can be bloody well used anybloodywhere in a sentence.

Blot. The anus. 'Sitting on my blot all day long'.

Blow. To achieve orgasm.

Blow job. Oral sex: A typically poor and inaccurate American expression.

Blow off. To fart.

Blowie. A blowfly. Also a despicable character.

Bludge. To live off the fat of the land, also Dole Bludger (to live off the unemployment benefit). On the bludge.

Bludger. Originally living off the earnings of prostitutes, which is why bludger is still a fighting word among older Australians.

Bludget. A female decoy for thieves, often masquerading as a prostitute (archaic).

Blue. A fight. 'I got in a real blue last night'. True blue. Loyal, faithful.

Blue-arsed fly. To run around like a blue-arsed fly. To run madly about achieving nothing.

Blue streak. A fast mover.

Blue vein. The penis. Hence Blue Veiner, an erection.

Bluebird. A policeman. Popular after blue uniforms were introduced in the 1930s.

'cop'

Bluey.
(1) A rolled blanket carried by a swagman (see Swaggie).
(2) A red-headed man's nickname.
(3) A summons. (From the original blue paper).

!?

Blurter. The anus. A wet fart.

ω/ω

Boat people. Refugees (usually Vietnamese) coming from south-east Asia and landing illegally.

rcs ?

Boat race. A rigged horse race. A form of beer drinking contest.

Bob Hope. Marijuana (dope, rhyming slang).

RS

Bodgie.
(1) Australian teddy boy of the fifties and early sixties. Wore bright clothes, ripple-soled shoes and pants pegged tight from the thighs down. Considered degenerate by all right-thinking people.
(2) Inferior, often worthless. A bodgie job (something thrown together in a hurry).

Bodgies Blood. A milk bar favourite of the bodgie era: Coca-Cola with strawberry syrup. Legend had it that an aspirin added to the Coke made it an aphrodisiac or, depending upon who told you the legend, a dexadrine substitute.

Body exchange. Singles bar.

Bog. The lavatory. Also boghouse. To do a bog/have a bog also implies producing a particularly impressive stool (see Turd).

Bogie. Snot.

Boiler. An older woman. Usually a well-worn prostitute. 'She's an old boiler'. Once applied with drastic industrial results by an airline owner of his hostesses.

Boiled dog. Affectation or pretentiousness.

Bollocks. The testicles. Also a mistake. More commonly used as 'he made a bollocks of that' (see Balls-up) or as a cheery expletive 'Oh, bollocks!'.

Bollocky. Naked. Standing in the bollocky.

Bolt. Shoot your bolt. To ejaculate.

Bombo. Cheap wine.

Bondi. Shoot through like a Bondi tram. To run off hurriedly.

Bong. A water pipe for smoking marijuana. To indulge in this habit is to bong on.

Bonk. To ejaculate.

Bonzer. Excellent! Terrific.

Boobs. Breasts.

Boofhead. An idiot, an oaf.

Boomer. A complicated ambitious lie.

Boong. (offensive). An Aborigine. Also any black man (see Gin). *yes*

Booze. Drink. Used as far back as 600 years ago to describe excessive drinking, an ancient and noble expression for an ancient and noble pastime.

Boozies. Breasts. ∞

Booze bus. Random breath testing vehicle.

Borrie. A turd. Surfing expression; can refer to faeces floating in the ocean or one produced as a result of personal effort.

Bot. A germ. Also a person always borrowing or scrounging. *6ελέμης*

Bottler. First class. Excellent.

Bottom-of-the-harbour. Popular tax evasion scheme where the records were dumped (often in the sea).

Boulders. Breasts. A brassiere is an over the shoulder boulder holder. ∞

Bower bird. A petty thief.

Box. The vagina. *o*

Brass monkey. Extremely cold. 'It would freeze the balls off a brass monkey'. In front of mum, the cautious son would say 'cold enough to freeze the walls off a grass humpy'. One fine explanation of the expression is that a brass monkey is a tray for cannonballs which slide off in cold weather due to variable coefficients of linear expansion. Or something.

Breakfast. All over the place like a mad woman's breakfast. Something scattered in every direction.

Breezer. A fart.

Brewer's droop. Sexual impotence caused by too much beer. (see Oyster).

Brick. Built like a brick shithouse. Well-built. Solid.

Bride. Off like a bride's nightie. A rapid transition from one state to another.

Bridge. Chuck a bridge. To show off one's underwear (usually of a woman).

Brothel creepers. Old-fashioned crepe-soled shoes.

Brown-eye. The anus. Usually to drop one's trousers in a passing car and show off the brown eye to another motorist. Not recommended when driving.

Brown-nose. A crawler. (see Arse-licker).

Brownout Romeo. During WWII when the streets were kept dark so cities could not be a target, the Brownout Romeo went around copping a cheap feel.

Brush. A young woman old enough to have pubic hair.

Buckley's. Buckley's hope or Buckley's chance. Next to no hope.

Buck's night. An all-male tradition of drunkeness and debauchery preceding a wedding. Traditionally the groom-to-be is left chained to a pole, given a guest role in a live sex show or otherwise embarrassed by his dearest friends.

Budgie cage. A police wagon with a *A Black Maria of sorts* canvas covered metal cage for prisoners.

Buff. Nudity. In the buff. *ΤϬΙΤϬΙΟΔ*

Bug rake. A comb.

Bugger. Usually endearing, occasionally malicious. Bugger it, bugger him, bugger the horses.
(1) Bugger about. To fool around.
(2) Bugger me dead. Exclamation of shock.
(3) Bugger off. To leave or an order to leave (see Piss off).
(4) Silly buggers. People who waste time on trivial things.
The word itself originates in a 500-year-old slur on the sexual habits of the Bulgars or Bulgarians.

Bugger-all. Very little.

Buggered. Worn-out.

Buggery.
(1) Go to buggery (see Piss off).
(2) Like buggery. Considerably. It stung like buggery.

Bull. Rubbish. Nonsensical talk.
(1) Bullshit. Complete claptrap.
(2) Bull(shit) artist. One who talks

bullshit.

(3) Policeman (uniformed).

• A rural expression for women who want to avoid pregnancy: 'It's not the bull they're afraid of, it's the calf'.

• **Bull's wool.** Nonsense.

Bum. The buttocks.
(1) Bum a ride. To hitch-hike.
(2) Bite your bum. An admonition, an indication to shut up.
(3) Take it up the bum. Of anal intercourse partners. Also a general expression meaning to accept the inevitable.

Bumbrusher. A military orderly.

Bumming off. Anal sex.

Bumf. Military gossip. Short for bumfluff (see Fluff).

Bumfluff. The first appearance of hair on the face of a young man; also used for the youth himself: 'G'day there bumfluff'.

Bumfreezer. Any short coat or jacket.

Bumpers. Breasts.

Bum chums. Close homosexual acquaintances.

Bumhole. The anus. Also a popular expression of abuse.

Bump and grind. Traditional choreography of a stripper or exotic dancer.

Bun. A buttered bun. A woman who

will willingly take part in group sex.

Bundle. Drop a bundle. To give birth.

Bung.
(1) Bunging it on. To behave
   erratically, to squabble.
(2) Bunging on side. To put on an
   affected manner.
(3) To go bung. To go bankrupt.

Bunghole. Cheese. So named for its
constipating effect: bunging up the
hole.

Bunny. A fool or victim. 'OK, I'll be
the bunny ... '

Buns. Sanitary napkins. A young
woman having her period is said to
have the buns on. That along with
lesbianism and frigidity is the only
acceptable reason for an Australian
woman not to have sex (see Little
White Mice).

Burn off. To outstrip someone in a
car, usually in an unofficial race away
from a set of traffic lights.

Burn the grass. Urinate outdoors.
Popular expression in the 1940s.

Burnt stick. Better than a poke in
the eye with a burnt stick. A less
painful alternative.

Bury. Bury the bishop. To have sex.
(see Pork sword).

Bushfire blonde. Woman with red
hair.

Bush oyster. A sheep's testicle.

Bush scrubber. A rural harlot.

Bushman's honk. Blowing the nose by placing a finger alternately over each nostril, scorning offers of handkerchiefs or tissues.

Bust
(1) A portion of the female anatomy noticeably lacking in fashion models.
(2) Bust your guts. To work hard.

Butch. Lesbian. Applied to the traditional masculine lesbian who had tattoos, wore Y-front underpants and could be relied on in a brawl, rather than the much less entertaining feminist lesbians of recent years.

Buttonhole. The clitoris.

C

Cab. First cab off the rank. The first person to move.

Cack-catchers. Trousers tied at the bottom, often with bowyangs (strings) when using farm equipment, or with bicycle clips.

Cactus. In the cactus. In trouble. Can also be used as carked: completely worn out or broken.

Cake. A harlot.

Call girl. A prostitute with a telephone.

Call of nature. The need to urinate.

Camp. Effeminate, homosexual. Also
(1) Camp it up. To exaggerate effeminate mannerisms.
(2) Camp as a row of tents. Obviously homosexual. Originally British theatrical slang and we know all about them!

Canaries. Derisive term for Australian convicts after yellow uniforms were introduced in the 1820s.

Cancer stick. Cigarette.

Captain Cook. Rhyming slang. A look. Also, a famous alternative nursery rhyme character: 'Captain Cook did a poop, behind the kitchen door/The cat came up and licked it up and hollered out for more'.

Cark. To die. He carked it last night.

Cat. A passive homosexual (see Receiver). Also:
(1) Go like a cut cat. To run very fast (as a cat would run after being cut: castrated).
(2) Let the cat out of the bag. To disclose secrets.

Catfight. A fight between two women.

Cathouse. A brothel.

Chair. In the chair, the person due to buy a round of drinks.

Charity moll. An amateur prostitute or a woman who gives her sexual favours for free. An outmoded but charming expression.

Cheat sheet. An expenses claim submitted by employee.

Cheeks. The buttocks.

Cherry.
(1) The maidenhead.
(2) Very small breasts.

Chew and spew. A cheap eating house.

Chiack. Cheek or impudence.

Chichi. Tiny breasts. (Original Japanese word adopted by occupation servicemen).

China. Form of address for a friend; from China Plate: Mate.

Chink. A person of Chinese extraction. Henry Lawson once wrote: 'Get a move upon the pigtails when you've got an hour to spare', reflecting on the habits of gold miners last century who would go out on Sundays for recreation and beat up a few Chinamen. Australians have always instinctively distrusted anyone who works harder than they do: Chinamen were no exception.

Chippy. A harlot.

Choc-a-block. Really full. Applies to social spaces such as pubs (the beer garden was choc-a-block) or women (Jonno was choc-a-block up her).

Chocolate frog. A wog (foreigner). Rhyming slang (see Gosford dog).

Chook. Chicken. Also the classic Australian phrase 'I hope your chooks turn to emus and kick your dunny down'.

Choozies. Affectionate term for breasts, used by children of all ages.

Chow. A Chinese person, most

frequently a restaurateur (chow is the Chinese word for food). The Chinese in Australia revenge themselves for years of discrimination by serving dreadful fried rice to drunks in their ubiquitous country town cafes (see Chew and Spew) and by refusing to translate the interesting dishes written on the wall in Chinese.

Christening. Like a prostitute at a christening. Out of place (See Bastard and Pork Chop).

Christmas hold. A handful of nuts. Used in wrestling when one opponent grabs the other by the testicles.

Chromo. A prostitute.

Chuck. To vomit. Also
(1) The big chuck. A long bout of
where's (2)? vomiting.
A popular Australian radio character of the 1970s was Chuck Chunder.

Chug-a-lug. To drink in one gulp. Often a feature of drinking contests, where the friends of the contestant gather around and chant the expression by way of encouragement.

Chunder. Vomit. (see Yawn). Popular since the 1950s, the word comes from the old English 'chunter', to mutter or grumble. Chunder should contain small pieces of tomato skin; vomitus lacking this vital ingredient should more properly be called spew.

Circle jerk. A contest involving a

group of young men who sit in a circle and masturbate. The winner is whoever finishes first.

Clam. The bearded clam. Female sex organs. Hence: Spear the bearded clam (intercourse).

Clam

Clap. Venereal disease.

Claytons. A substitute. From TV commercial urging drinkers to have a Clayton's (non-alcoholic drink). 'The drink you have when you don't have a drink'.

Clever dick. A know-all.

Clock. A blow with the fist. 'I clocked him one'.

Closet queen. A secret or closet homosexual.

Clucky. Very keen to have a baby. Chooks cluck a lot when they are sitting on a clutch of eggs.

Cock. The penis. Not strictly one of the great Four Letter Words, as only the sexual aspect of cock is considered taboo.

Cock-up. A mistake (see Balls-up).

Cocktails. Diarrhoea.

Coconuts.
(1) Breasts (from the song Luvverly Buncha).
(2) Testicles.

Cods. Testicles.

Cocksucker. Homosexual (US).

Cockteaser. A tease, a girl who leads men on.

Combo. A person of mixed European/Aboriginal parentage; expression comes from the 1890s and is uncharacteristically polite.

Come.
(1) Come across. To give sexual favours.
(2) Come out (of the closet) to publicly admit being homosexual.
(3) To achieve orgasm.

m

Comic cuts. Guts (rhyming slang).

RS

Commo. Member of a communist party. All-purpose term of derision for anyone less conservative than the speaker.

Contemplate the navel. To daydream.

Cornstalk. Early term for a colonial: Australian born, Australian bred/long in the legs and thick in the head.

rcs

Cottage. A public lavatory popular with homosexuals.

Country member. Parliamentary representative from a rural electorate. The traditional Australian response to a politician who says proudly: 'I'm a Country member,' is 'Yes, we remember'.

Cowyard confetti. Bullshit.

Crack.
(1) Crack a fat. To attain an erection.
(2) Crack a shitty. To lose one's temper.
(3) Crack on to. To pick up a member of the opposite sex.
(4) To crack it. To succeed, usually in sexual matters. Also neg: 'He couldn't crack it with a whore'.

Cradle snatcher. A person who shows an unhealthy interest in a very young person.

Crap. Excrement. (see Shit).
Originally the dregs in a wine barrel; used by people too polite to say shit but linked to excretory functions through cistern manufacturer Thomas Crapper.

Crash. Bowel movement. One 'has a crash'.

Crash hot. Great, terrific, wonderful. (See Shit hot).

Cream one's jeans. To have an orgasm while dressed.

Creek.
(1) Up shit creek. In trouble.
(2) Up shit creek without a paddle. In worse trouble.

Cremie. Person of mixed Aboriginal/European race. An expression from the 1880s which gives a fair idea of the social life of the 1860s and 70s.

Crook. Unhealthy. A crook job, feeling crook. Also to put someone crook: to give wrong advice.

Crow.
(1) Stone the crows. Exclamation of surprise.
(2) The day the crow (eagle) shits. Pay day.
(3) An unattractive woman.
(4) A nun. Due to the black habits,

nuns were often called Old Black Crows (but not to their faces or you would get a good whack on the knuckles with a ruler).

Cruiser. Old style 20oz beer glass.

Cruising. Looking for a sex partner, usually on a bar crawl (see Body exchange).

Crutch rot. A coating of grime, sweat and fungal infection that collects between the legs of men living communally in military or educational establishments; exacerbated by cold winter mornings and shared, but under-utilised, shower facilities.

Cunt. Female pudendum. More commonly a term of extreme derision mainly used about men. He's a stupid cunt. While a woman may, on occasion, be called a cunt, she will never be called a prick.

o

cf. Fr. con

good point

Cunthooks. Fingers. An unfriendly nickname. While you would describe someone in their absence as bastard you would not call them cunthooks unless they were there. One of the great fighting words in the Australian vocabulary.

fighting word

Curl a mo. Expression of approval, implying that the successful person can stand back and preen by curling the ends of his moustache.

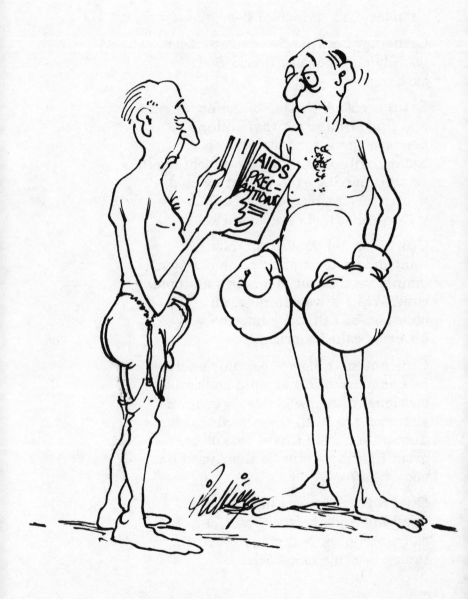

Dung puncher

Daisy chain. A group of males all engaged in intercourse.

Dag, daggy. A stupid or, sometimes, droll person. Rural term for sheepshit.

Dangler. A flasher. A man who exposes his sexual organ to women in public. In reply to the traditional call of 'Do you know what this is love?' the astute woman will answer: 'Well, it looks like a prick only smaller'.

Darkie. A turd. To choke a darkie: to defecate.

Dark meat. An Aboriginal woman.

Date. The anus.

Date mate. A homosexual (see Bum chum, Poophole pal).

Date roll. A roll of toilet paper. (See Pakapoo Tickets).

Dead Exhausted. Also, obvious.
(1) Dead giveaway. Totally obvious.

(2) Dead loss. Complete loss.

(3) Dead from the shoulders up. Dense, obtuse.

(4) Dead set. Absolutely true.

(5) Dead to the world. Heavily asleep.

Deadshit. A thoroughly despicable person.

Decrapitation. Breaking wind. A famous party record, the International Decrapitation Contests, featuring Australian champion Paul Boomer. The narration of this classic is often attributed, erroneously, to Jack Davey.

De facto. A man who goes to live with a woman whose marriage has broken up because he does not have children of his own to abuse.

Deknacker. To castrate.

Demon. A plainclothes detective. Last century the expression began as just D, became Dee, then Demon. Detectives do not resist this nickname for fear of being called something worse. Not to be confused with the Demon Drink which is everybody's tipple, not restricted to police.

Derro. A derelict homeless man, usually alcholic.

Dick. Penis. Originated last century as army slang.

(1) Had the dick. To be ruined.

(2) Clever dick. Know-all.

(3) Dickhead. A fool or an idiot.

In mixed company one may use 'had

the Richard' but Clever Richard or Richardhead will be received with the scorn they deserve.

Dickless Tracy. A policewoman.

Diddle.
(1) The penis.
(2) To have sexual intercourse.
(3) To con someone: diddle them out of their money.

Didee. The toilet. From an early American word for diaper which is what they called nappies.

Diddleums. Delerium tremens.

Dine at the Y. To engage in cunnilingus.

Ding. An Italian.

Dingbat. A Chinese.

Dingbats. Stupid or silly.

Dingo. A coward, a low character. As in 'put on a dingo act'.

Dingo breath. A virulent form of halitosis.

Dipshit. A person suspected of having a prediliction for anal intercourse.

Dipstick. The penis. Also usable as an insult: 'G'day dipstick'.

Dip the wick. To have sexual intercourse.

Dirty. He did the dirty on us. He cheated.

Dirty weekend. A short period of

illicit sexual activity.

Dirty work at the crossroads.
Sexual intercourse.

Dog's bottom. A term of approval. 'Is he dog's bottom? Too right!'

Dog's breakfast. Great confusion (cf Madwoman's breakfast).

Dog's cock. An exclamation mark! (journalistic slang).

Dog's dick. A more personal variant of the 40-foot barge pole, when applied to a noxiously unattractive or assertive woman: 'I wouldn't fuck her with a dog's dick'.

Dog's dick red. A colour between salmon and magenta.

Dog's vomit. Unappetising food.

Domain cocktail. A drink of petrol and pepper, or methylated spirits, boot polish, flytox.

Donald Duck or a Donald. n. A fuck (rhyming slang). See also Wellington.

Dong. A blow. To dong him one, to hit him.

Donger. The penis. An affectionate term implying size and utility. Not used as an insult.

Donnybrook. An all-in brawl, commonly at a set event such as a football match. Donnybrook is an Irish town whose fairs used to be a bit riotous.

Donk. A fool. Also, a penis. Also a car engine.

Doodle. The penis.

Double bummer. A woman (referring to the dual orifices).

Dougnnut. The golden doughnut, female sex organs.

Down.
(1) Go down on. To engage in oral sex.
(2) Down the gurgler/plughole. Lost, wasted effort.

Drag. Women's clothes worn by men.

Drag queen. A homosexual who wears women's clothing.

Drilling for Vegemite. n A homosexual act (see Transmitter).

Dropkick. A cunt (as term of abuse not in reference to female genitalia). Rhyming football slang: Dropkick and punt.

Drop your daks. Take off your trousers.

Drop your gear. Instruction given to a woman to undress quickly in readiness for sexual activity.

Drop one's load. To ejaculate.

Drop your lunch. To produce a substantial fart.

Drop the soap. What a sensible heterosexual never does if sharing a shower with someone who may be a poofter. Why they are sharing in the first place is another matter.

Drop your guts. To fart.

Dry. Dry as a Pommy's towel. As dry as you can get! Also 'dry as a nun's nasty'. Also 'as dry as a kookaburra's khyber.' (Khyber Pass: arse. rhyming slang).

Dry rooting. To engage in the motions of sexual intercourse while clothed.

Dubbo. A rural fool, a bumpkin. From any country town not necesarily Dubbo.

Ducks and drakes. The alcoholic shakes (see also Joe Blakes).

Dung puncher. A homosexual (see Transmitter).

Dunny. An outside toilet.

Dutch oven. A practical joke played in bed. The party of the first part pulls the blanket over the head of the party of the second part, then the party of the first part farts.

Dyke.
(1) A lesbian. (US).
(2) A toilet. Australian school and army slang from the 1920s.

Each way. n. To bet win and place.
Also bi-sexual. *bi*

Eagle. The day the eagle shits :
payday (see Crow).

Eat. To engage in oral sex.

Eat shit. To be submissive.

Edgar Britt. Shit. Rhyming slang *RS*
after a famous jockey.

Eff off. Euphemism for fuck off.

Elders. Breasts. *∞*

Eligible bachelor. Media euphemism
for an old poof who is available to
squire women on social occasions.

Empty. An orgasm. As in 'To have an *⌇*
empty'.

Endless belt. A prostitute.

End. Get one's end in (of a man) to *φ*
have sex.

Ethnic. An expression officially *rcs*

introduced to supersede derogatory terms for the migrant communities in Australia. Gleefully adopted as a handy, all-encompassing term of abuse for ALL foreigners. This is known as simplifying the language.

Equipment. The male sex organs.

Exhaust pipe. The anus.

Eyeful. An attractive woman.

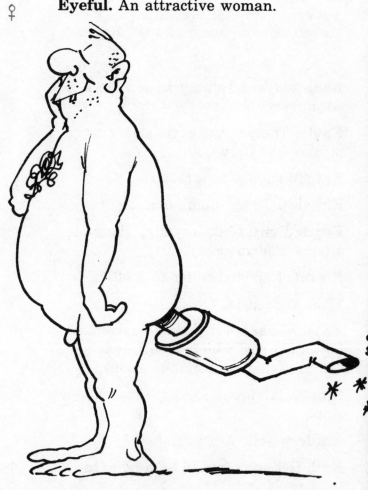

Exhaust pipe

F. Euphemism for Fuck. (see Eff off).

Face. Off your face. Obliterated by drugs/alcohol.

Fag. A homosexual. A cigarette.

Fag hag. A woman who associates with homosexual men.

Fair.
(1) Fair suck of the sav (saveloy).
(2) Fair crack of the whip.
(3) Fair and square.
(4) Fair shake of the dice.

Fairy. Homosexual. To shoot a fairy: To fart.

Fall off the back of a truck. To be gained by illegal means.

Fall on your arse. To make a major error.

Family jewels. The male sex organs.

Fanny. The vagina. Americans cause great mirth in Australia because they use the word to describe buttocks. The expression has been common for more than a century and comes from the literary character Fanny Hill.

Fart.
(1) To break wind via the anus. A fine old English word, used in literature for about eight centuries. (Warning: modern English teachers are rarely swayed by this argument from scholars who wish to use the word in school essays).
(2) Stupid old fart. A foolish person.
(3) A little fart. A stupid young person.

Fart about. To waste time.

Farting in a lift. The lowest form of social behaviour where the farter leaves the lift immediately having done his damage. Only the graffiti scrawler and the donkey voter are as lowly as someone who would fart in a lift: all three irrevocably linked by their pathetic anonymity.

Fart-arse. To waste time. Fart-arsing about.

Fart-sack. A sleeping bag.

Fat guts. Term of address for an overweight person.

Fatso. A more intimate term of address than Fat guts.

Fat. An erection (see Crack).

Feature. To have sexual intercourse.

Features. Jovial term of address, short for Cuntfeatures.

Federating. Copulating.

Ferret. Penis as in
(1) Give the ferret a run.
(2) Run the ferret up the drainpipe. To
    engage in sex.

Ferry. A prostitute.

Fiancee. A woman engaged but never subsequently married to a notorious fairy. (See Closet queen).

Fingering. The manual stimulation of the female sex organs, frequently performed in picture theatres in the 1950s and 60s. Hence Finger stalls, the back row of the cinema.

Five finger discount. Shoplifting.

Five Finger Mary. The hand, as a masturbatory organ.

Fizzgig. A police informer.

Flag. To have the flags out. Menstruation.

Flake. To collapse either from drinking or exhaustion. Flake out.

Flash as a rat with a gold tooth. Inappropriately overdressed, overconfident, overdone.

Flasher. A man who exposes his genitals in public.

Flat out. Busy.
Flat out like a lizard drinking. Extremely busy.

Fleas and itches. Pictures (movies): rhyming slang.

Flea pit. Front section of movie theatre.

Flick. Give someone the flick: to reject or dismiss someone. Also flick pass: the arse (the rhyming slang).

Flog the log. To masturbate.

Fluff. Originally meant to fart (WWII slang). Now means to make a mistake: to fluff your lines.

Fly.
(1) To fly a kite. To cash a worthless cheque, or to propose a scheme with no intention of carrying it through.
(2) No flies on him. Someone who is not easily fooled. A sharp operator.

Flybog. Jam.

Flynn. In like Flynn. (After Errol Flynn). A successful move, often in sex.

Four letter word. Polite euphemism for the major Anglo-Saxon taboo words Fuck and Cunt.

Franger. A condom.

Frat. To have sex with the locals. Originally military slang; troops were warned not to fraternise.

Fred Nerk. An imaginary character regarded as the ultimate idiot (see also Blind Freddy).

Freebie. A free item (often sex from a prostitute).

French. Obscene language. One who accidentally uses inappropriate language in front of women will say 'excuse my French'.

French bath. Washing only the bits that have been used for sexual intercourse before going home to the wife. Superseded in recent years by the spread of gymnasiums; it is no longer necessary to explain why you have had a shower on the way home.

Frenchy. A condom. From French letter. Many mothers warn their daughters to watch out for the telltale ring showing in the wallet that indicates their boy scout of the moment may be a little bit too prepared. Classic Australian verse: 'The boy stood on the burning deck/He wished he'd never been born/His mother said he wouldn't be/If the Frenchy hadn't torn'.

Frig. To have sexual intercourse. From the original frigging about: messing about aimlessly. Now used as a polite replacement for fuck. A popular chorus goes: 'Frigging in the rigging (repeated twice), cause there's fuck-all else to do'. Often sung to alleviate boredom.

Frig-up. A blunder.

Frog. A condom. Also: frogskin.

Front.
(1) Bravado. As in 'More front than Myers/Foys' etc meaning to have a big front or a lot of bravado.
(2) To approach a woman re a sexual liaison, or to accompany a woman to a dance or party, thus indicating to one's friends that a conquest has been made.

Front bum. The vagina.

Fuck. To have sexual intercourse.
(1) Fuck about. To act the fool.
(2) Fuck up. To ruin.
(3) Fuck off. An exclamation or order to depart.
(4) What the fuck! Who cares ...
(5) Don't give a fuck. To not care about a result.
(6) Fuck-all. Very little. An even tinier amount is 3/8ths of 5/8ths of fuck-all.
(7) Fuck you. American way of saying get fucked. This all-purpose obscenity does not solely imply sex. As a curse, wishing someone fucked also implies that they should be utterly confused and defeated. In past centuries to curse someone was not just an expression of dislike, it was to call on some force of nature or a spirit to aid you in wishing ill upon them. Modern cursing is more a matter of emphasis than belief.

Fucked. Exhausted, damaged, useless, broken.

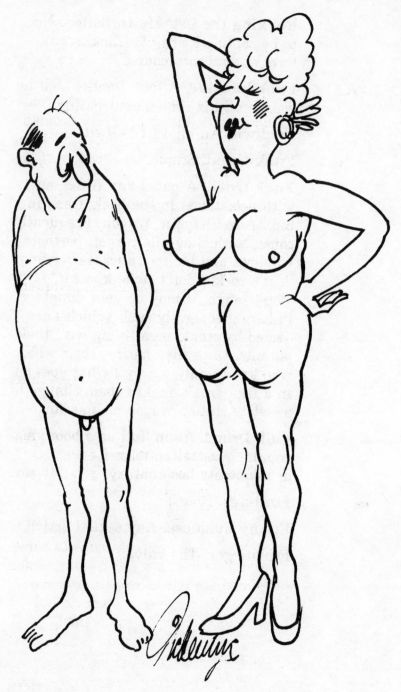

Front bum

Fucking the fist. Masturbation. Not to be confused with fist fucking, a form of anal intercourse.

μαλάκας

Fuck-knuckle. A fool. Implies that he wastes all his time masturbating.

Fuckwit. An idiot (cf halfwit).

Fuckwitted. Stupid.

Fuck truck. A panel van fitted out with a mattress in the back. (see Sin bin). Also Shaggin' Wagon. Frequently comes with shag pile carpet, porthole windows and bumper stickers reading: 'If it's rockin don't come knockin' OR 'don't laugh, it may be your daughter in here'. Generally such vehicles are owned by single men living with their parents. Once they marry, their wife, who knows only too well what goes on in a fuck truck, makes them change to a sedate station wagon or a sedan.

cf. Scand. full

Full. Drunk. As in 'full as a boot'. A popular Australian term for drunkenness last century.

Funbags. Breasts.

Funny business. Any sexual activity.

Furburger. The vulva.

G

Galah. A fool or an idiot.

Game.
(1) Prostitution. On the game meaning involved in prostitution.
(2) Brave in the face of obstacles: As game as Ned Kelly.

Gang bang. A group of men having sex with one woman. (See Train, Onion). Also gangie. Traditionally the first man will seduce the girl then ask 'what about my mates?' on the assumption that no woman could bring herself to break the close bonds that exist between an Australian male and his peer group.

Garbage guts. A person who eats to excess.

Gash. A woman or her vagina: one of the less flattering dysphemisms.

Gay. A homosexual.

Gazob. A fool.

Gazungas. Breasts.

Gazunta.

(1) Any item of hardware whose name is not known like a doover or a whatsie but frequently refers to a chamber pot which gazunta the bed.

(2) The genitals.

Gear. Clothing.

(1) Drop one's gear. To undress usually in public at a party.

(2) Get your gear on. To dress hurriedly.

Getting your oats. Achieving a successful sexual liaison.

Giblets. The sternum. You can punch someone in the giblets. He may complain later of a punch in the guts: giblets tend to belong to other people.

Gig. A fool, one who acts inappropriately.

Giggle factory. Lunatic asylum.

Giggle water. Champagne or any other sparkling wine (the sweeter the better) which in Australia acts as an aphrodisiac on women but gives men the gutsache. (See Lolly Water).

Gin. An Aboriginal woman (derog).

Gin burglar/Gin jockey. A white man who has sex with Aboriginal women.

Gin's piss. Weak beer.

Girls' week. The menstrual period.

Give her one. To present a woman with the ultimate gift: the body and soul of an Australian man, in that order.

Give someone the drum. To give advice. To give a tip (horseracing).

Glad eye. A flirtatious glance.

Glum bum. A pessimist.

Go down on. To perform oral sex.

Go to the throttling pit. A visit to a urinal.

Goat. A lecherous man.

Gob. To expectorate.

Gobbler. Woman who is available to perform oral sex, often on more than one man at a sitting. The gobbler exists more as a figment of the collective male imagination but that does not stop a group of men making gobble-gobble noises as a notorious Slag or Rough Moll passes them, invariably causing great hilarity.

Goanna. Piano (Pianna) rhyming slang.

RS

Goer. A seemingly promiscuous, or at least available, woman.

(♀)

Gold digger. A woman who seeks to profit socially or financially from the judicious disbursement of her physical charms.

(♀)

Golly. A large gob of spit often ejected by the compressed air method (deep breath, curl spit on to tongue and puff cheeks while spitting). Probably derived from gollywog (see Wog).

Gong. Opium.

Good time girl. One who seeks enjoyment while forfeiting responsibility.

Good on you. Typical Australian expression of approval. Originally a blessing: God On You. There may be something slightly blasphemous about using it in a non-spiritual context, such as a TV commercial.

Goody-goody. An excessively virtuous person.

Goof. A fool.

Goog. An egg. Full as a goog: extremely drunk.

Goolies. Testicles. To spit or a gob of spit.

Goomie. A metho drinker.

Goop. A fool.

Goose. A clumsy fool.

Gooseberry. Playing gooseberry, to cramp someone's style, to hang around a couple who want to be alone.

Gorgeous gussies. Frilly underwear, introduced as a fashion item by tennis player Gussie Moran.

Gormless. Stupid.

Gosford dog. A wog. Foreigner. Rhyming slang.

Grab by the balls. To impress strongly.

Grapefruit. Breasts.

Grassfighter. A brawler (Depression era term).

Grass widow. A woman whose husband is temporarily absent.

(♀) *gräsänka*

Gravel rash. Said to be suffered by crawlers or sycophants.

Greaser. A crawler or a toady.

Greek. Greek style. Anal intercourse.

ψ

Greenie. A richly-hued blob of spit.

Grind. To indulge in vigorous sexual intercourse.

φ

Grommet. The vagina. Can be used as term of abuse (you little grommet) or as a term to indicate intercourse.

o
φ

Grizzleguts. Someone constantly complaining.

Grot. A person who lives in messy surroundings, or the surroundings themselves. From an old Anglo-Saxon word meaning tiny particles.

Group grope. Mutual sex by three or more people.

Grog on. To continue drinking for an extended period, a description of public communal drinking.

Grope. Sexual fondling.

Groupie. A girl who makes herself sexually available to members of a

(♀)

(rock) group.

(♀) **Grunter.** A woman available for sexual activity. Usually one who otherwise makes no major social demands such as phone calls, conversation or the name of the gentleman concerned.

rcs **Gub.** A white person. This disrespectful Aboriginal term (called getting their own back) is also pronounced gubber or gubbo.

(♀) **Gunnie.** A girl who goes off with a bang.

Gumsuckling. Kissing.

Gunk. Junkfood.

ω̭ **Gurk.** To break wind, fart.

Gussie. An effeminate man.

Gut-buster. Activity requiring a lot of effort.

Gutful. A sufficiency.

Gutless wonder. A disappointing performer.

Gutrot. Cheap and dangerous alcohol.

Guts.
(1) Hate someone's guts. To detest them.
(2) Have someone's guts for garters. To get revenge.
(3) Hold one's guts. To keep quiet.
(4) Spill your guts. To reveal information.

Gutsache.
(1) A sore stomach.
(2) Someone who is perpetually complaining.

Gutser. To come a gutser. To take a tumble.

Guzzle. To eat or drink greedily.

Guzzleguts. An indiscriminate gastronome.

Gyp. To cheat or swindle.

< rcs

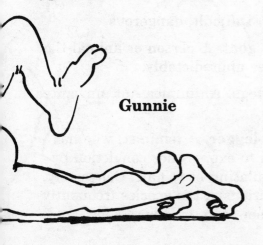

Gunnie

H

Hack. To spit. Also a common variety of journalist.

Hades. Hell. Go to Hades is still considered a nice, creative, medium-strength curse.

Hair
(1) The short and curlies (pubic hairs).
(2) Hair of the dog that bit you. An alcoholic (usually morning) drink to get rid of a hangover.
(3) Hair pie. Cunnilingus.

Hairy. Difficult, dangerous.

Hairy goat. A person or animal that behaves unpredictably.

Hairylegs. An unpleasant, unwanted person.

Hairy-legger. A feminist, who has chosen to express her conviction by accumulating body hair. Conversely, and curiously, the species frequently crops her scalp hair very short.

Half a yard of blue vein in the bloodhole. Sexual intercourse.

Hambone. A public strip act by a male. Usually the result of a drunken dare rather than a deep-seated desire to titillate.

Hairylegs

Hammocks. Medium-sized breasts.

Handbook. A magazine with pictures of nude women, used as a masturbatory aid.

Handbag. A homosexual man who accompanies a woman to social events; his value is purely decorative.

Hand job. Manual masturbation of a male by an obliging female.

Hanky panky. See Funny business.

Hard.
(1) Get a hard on. To maintain an erection.
(2) Put the hard word on. To ask someone for sexual intercourse.

Hard stuff. Drinks with a high alcohol content. Spirits.

Harry. An earnest amateur, a hanger-on. Invariably boring but available, may be of either sex. Most commonly found in artistic circles: a Theatre Harry.

Hawk the fork. To be a prostitute. Also hawk the dot (Old Aust).

Hayseed. A country bumpkin.

Headlights. Breasts.

Head. A dunny on a boat. Under NO circumstances get confused with Give Head (see Blow Job).

Heart-starter. An early morning drink to offset a hangover. (see Hair).

Heave. To vomit or dry-retch.

Heavy.
(1) Come the heavy. A man who tries to push a woman into sex.
(2) A bouncer at a nightspot whose occupation is to maintain the tone of the establishment by punching shit out of anyone improperly dressed. (And you thought fashion standards were set by a bunch of fairy designers!)

Heebie jeebies. Delerium tremens.

Heifer. A teenage girl.   (♀)

Hellhole. A rotten place.

Hen. A woman.   ♀

Hen's night. An outing by a group of women to celebrate the impending marriage of one of their number (cf Buck's Night).

Henry the Third. Turd. Rhyming   RS ⌒
slang: cf (Edgar).

Hey diddle diddle. A piddle   RS
(rhyming slang - of course!)

Hickey. Love bite (American).

Hide the sausage. Sexual   ♂
intercourse, not to be confused with a party game.

High. Drunk or stoned.

Hit and miss. Piss (rhyming slang).   RS

Hit the piss. To launch into a drinking bout.

Hock. A homosexual.

Hog. A greedy person.

Hoick. To clear the throat and spit.

Honeymooners' disease. Cystitis, a bladder condition that may coincide with the first extended period of sexual activity which, for a very small minority, is still the honeymoon.

Honey pot. The female pudendum.

Honey dipper. A latrine cleaner.

Hooker. A prostitute or call girl. This uninspired American euphemism comes from a Civil War General Hooker whose staff frequented the brothel area of Washington.

Hooks. A nickname or greeting, the publicly usable form of Cunthooks.

Hoon. A lout or yobbo, originally one who lived off earnings of a prostitute, now in general use. The hoon usually travels in a group.

Honk. A bad smell.

Hooch. Liquor.

Horn. An erect penis.

Horny. In the mood for romance.

Horseshit. Nonsense (see Bullshit).

Horse's hoof. Poof (rhyming slang).

Hots. To have the hots. To feel a strong sexual pull.

Hot cack. Good, excellent.

Hot shit. Excellent, good.

Hot stuff. A person who is sexually exciting.

House that Jack built. A clinic or hospital for venereal disease.

Hubcap bitter. A woman who rates her male companion according to the quality of his motor vehicle.

Huey. God. A generalised supreme being with particular responsibility for the weather. An Australian wanting rain, or good surf, will pray 'send 'er down Huey'. Australians are the only people in the world on first name terms with God.

Hum. To fart.

Humdinger. An excellent or impressive fart, so powerful that it resonates against the nearest hard surface: dingggg!. Also used as a general term of approval.

Hung like a horse. Fortunately blessed in the genital department.

Hunk. A sexually attractive man.

Hurl. To vomit.

Hustler. A male or female prostitute. (American).

Iron balls

/

Icy cold. A can of beer.

Ikey Mo. A Jew (from Isaac Moses).　ᴦᴄˢ

Imbo. An imbecile.

Inked. Drunk. A popular description from the 1890s.

Insect. Used as a term of abuse to indicate a small insignificant creature.

In the flowers. Menstruating.

Iron yourself out. To get drunk.

Iron balls. Tough, vigorous, strong.

Iron maiden. An authoritative stern woman.　(♀)

J

J Arthur. To masturbate. Rhyming slang from wank: J. Arthur Rank!

Jack. Venereal disease.

Jack off. To masturbate

Jacksie. Brothel.

Jacksy. The backside. Sitting around on your jacksy.

Jade. A sluttish woman (old English expression).

Jagged. Drunk.

Jagging. Gatecrashing parties.

Jail-bait. A girl under the legal age of sexual consent.

Jakes. A toilet.

Jam tart. A female. Also a fart (rhyming slang).

Jane. A woman.

Jap. Common abbreviation for a

Japanese, used with particular vitriol in Australia during and after World War II.

Jap crap. A Japanese motorcycle. Some purists still insist on American or British machines.

Jaybird. One who performs household and domestic duties naked.

Jerk off. To masturbate.

Jerrydiddle. A free drink.

Jerry pot. A chamber pot. A classical practical joke is to send out the victim to buy tinned cherries. The shopkeeper, who is in on the joke, will eventually supply a tin Jerry.

Jesus-freak. A religious extremist. (cf Bible-basher).

Jewish pianola. Cash register. < rcs

Jig. To play truant or wag school.

Jig a jig. Sexual intercourse, once φ
assumed to be the only expression used by foreigners for intimate congress.

Jiggery-pokery. Tricky dealings.

Jim jams. Misery or depression.

Jimmy Brits. Diarrhoea. Rhyming RS
slang. Also Edgar Britts.

Jimmy Riddle. A piddle, again RS
rhyming slang.

Joan of Arc. Shark. Rhyming slang. RS
More commonly Noah's (Noah's Ark).

Jobbie. A bowel movement.

The Joes. Misery, anguish, depression.

Joe Blake. Snake (rhyming slang).

Joe Blakes. The (alcoholic) shakes.

Joey. A sodomite, fop, hermaphrodite.

John. Prostitute's client. (US chiefly).

John Hunt. Cunt (rhyming slang). Politicians with this surname may pick up the nickname Rhyming Slang, as may normal human beings. Politicians aside, the nickname is usually in jest.

John Thomas. Penis. Coy American slang favoured by people who want us to know they have seen the US of A. We can tell what bits they saw most of.

Johnny Bliss. Piss. More rhyming slang. (An art form noted as much for its persistence as its inventiveness.)

Joe's witnesses. Members of the Jehovah's Witnesses, a religious sect renowned for door-to-door evangelism. By extension any door-knocking Bible-basher may be assumed to be a 'bloody Joe's Witness'.

Jollop. A laxative.

Judy. A woman (from Punch and).

Jugs. Breasts.

Juice freak. An enthusiastic consumer of alcohol.

Jump.
(1) Jump the gun. Start prematurely.
(2) One jump ahead. At an advantage.
(3) Take a running jump. Go away.
(4) To have intercourse.

Jump start. To initiate sex with assistance. When an older man takes up with a much younger woman it may be suggested he enlist the help of Mel Gibson and a set of jumper leads.

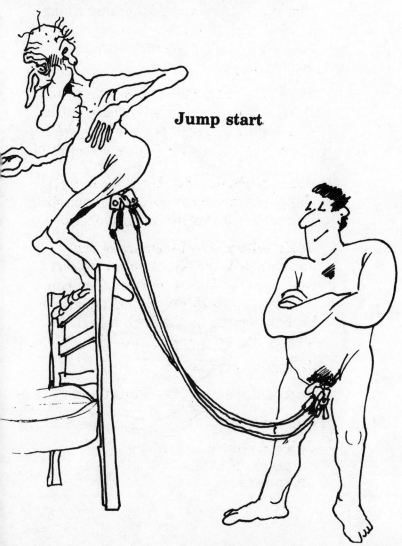

Jump start.

Jumper. Polite substitute for bum when telling someone to stick something up it.

Jungle bunny. Used to describe Aborigines and Pacific Islanders.

Jungle juice. Home brewed alcohol, often made from fermented potato peelings during World War II.

Kangaroo

Kangaroo. To defecate while squatting outdoors or to perch Asian style over a dubious toilet seat to avoid sitting on it. A useful skill for those who frequent rough pubs where the graffiti will often warn: 'Do not stand upon the seat/the crabs in here jump fifteen feet'.

Kangaroos in the top paddock. Daft, barmy, mad.

Kark. To die or break down.

Keister. The anus. Originally underworld slang for the body cavity as a hiding place for drugs and valuables. Popularised as a polite term for the backside by Americans.

ω

Kelly. A prostitute.

Kewpie. A prostitute. Rhyming slang: Kewpie Doll/Moll.

(♀) RS

Khyber. Arse. Khyber Pass/Arse.

ω RS

Kick the bucket. To die.

Kick in the arse. An unexpected setback.

Kick the cat. Transfer of aggression from a human being to the nearest dumb animal or inanimate object.

Kiddy. A small child, viewed sentimentally. To engage in the popular craze of family annihilation two or more kiddies are required. You never hear of the multiple death of a father, mother and only child.

rcs

RS

Kike. A person of the Jewish faith. Also Red Sea Pedestrian (always used fondly) or Four-by-Two (rhyming for Jew). The latter can be abbreviated to Fourby. The egalitarianism of Australia is easily demonstrated by the presence of nicknames, terms of abuse or dysphemisms for all segments of society, regardless of race, sex, physical handicap or intellectual capacity.

Kill a snake. To urinate.

King hit. To knock someone unconcious.

Kink. Any sexual deviation or attempt at variety in sexual activity.

Kip. A short sleep or nap. Originally a brothel where only a brief sleep was allowed.

Kiss and ride. The act of depositing a husband at a railway station, performed by a wife driving the family car and wearing a dressing gown. Curlers optional.

Kiss my arse. Expression of contempt.

•**Kising your sister.** Total anti-climax. 'Coming second in a race is like kissing your sister'.

Knackers. Testicles. ∞

Kneetrembler. Sexual intercourse with both parties standing. Also a Wallie (up against a wall).

Knickers in a twist. To be upset, agitated, panic-stricken.

Knob. The penis. Or more accurately the head of same.

Knock.
(1) To Knock. To criticise harshly.
(2) Knocked back. Sexual advances rejected.
•(3) Knocked up. Tired (unlike US ≠ US where it means pregnant).
(5) Knock back a few. To drink usually to excess.

Knockback. Rejection of sexual advances.

Knocker. Persistent critic. Opposition to any wacko scheme of any ruling political party is attributed to knockers, ineffectual malcontents or professional protesters.

Knockers. Breasts. ∞

Knocking shop. Brothel.

Knockover. A sure thing, an easy lay, a pushover.

Know someone in the Biblical sense. Have sexual intercourse.

Knucklehead. A clod, bonebrain, idiot.

Knuckle sandwich. A punch in the mouth.

Kook. A harmless, sometimes amusing, eccentric.

Koorie. An Aborigine.

rcs

Little man in the boat

L

La. A toilet. Also lala.

Lad. A rogue. A man who plays up.

Lady Jane. The vagina, one of many terms from the Victorian era. A certain Rolling Stones song, which a large and dreary subsection of the community assumed to be about marijuana, looks rather interesting in the light of this knowledge. Another popular name for the vagina was Daisy, which may be the reason our grandparents always put extra enthusiasm into singing 'Daisy, Daisy, give me your answer do'.

Lardhead. A fool.

Lady Muck. A woman who puts on airs and graces.

Lair. A flashy man.

Lairise. To behave like a lair. To lair it up; to come the lair.

Lairy. Flashy.

(rcs)

Land of the wrong white crowd.
New Zealand (Corruption of land of
the long white cloud).

Language. What one must watch
carefully in Mixed Company, for fear
of getting into a fight with the type of
fellow who uses defence of female
delicacy as an excuse to start a brawl.
Aggressive husbands will cross a
crowded room to shape up to someone
whose vulgar expressions have
ostensibly offended their spouses.

RS galore

La Perouse. Booze (yet again the old
rhyming slang): 'Let's go to the
rubbedy dub (pub), cash a Gregory
(Peck — cheque), buy some La Perouse
and get Mozart (Mozart and Lizst —
pissed)'.

Larrup. To beat someone up.

Larrikin. A wild young man, a lout, a
Street Arab. Popularly supposed to
derive from 'larkin about' and thought
to be an Irish expression but actually
an old English dialect word.

Larry Dooley. A beating. To give
someone Larry Dooley.

Lash.
(1) A thrillseeking excursion, probably
    including sex, alcohol and fast
    motor vehicles.
(2) An attempt at something. In early
    Australia, overseers used to argue
    over who would get to flog the
    convicts, saying: 'Let me have a
    lash'.

Laughing juice. Alcohol.

Lavo. A lavatory.

Lay. To have sexual intercourse, or a woman who is good/available.   ♀ (♀)

Lazy as Lumley's dog. Extremely lazy. The apocryphal mutt in question had to lean against a wall to bark.

Lead.
(1) Go down like a lead balloon. To fail.
(2) Put lead in your pencil. To increase (male) sex drive.

Leak. To urinate.

Leanaway. A drunkard.

Leery of the brush. A man wary of marriage.

Left footer. A Roman Catholic. Why?

Leghorn. A woman who plays lawn bowls. Known as White Leghorns due to the traditional white uniforms and greeted by the uncouth with cries of 'chook, chook, chook'.

Leg-opener. Any alcohol. In the belief that a few drinks lowers resistance. Classic leg-openers include Pimms No. 1 Cup, Sparkling Porphry Pearl, Port and Coke, Blackberry Nip. In fact, any drink in which the alcohol can be disguised. In inexperienced hands the injudicious use of a leg-opener can result in an incredibly drunk woman almost impossible to pour into a taxi.

Lemonhead. A surfboard rider who

uses lemon juice to bleach his hair for an instant outdoors image.

Lemon avenue. A female teetotaller.

Lemons. Breasts.

Length. To slip her a length. To have sexual intercourse.

Let the dog see the bunny. An invitation to a woman to show herself naked to ensure immediate readiness and enthusiasm in the man.

Letting off. Farting.

Lezzy. A lesbian. Also, lezzo. Two women showing public affection in Australia may be greeted with knowing cries of 'Les be friends'. In general there are very few terms for lesbian in the Australian idiom; Australian men find lesbians almost impossible to come to grips with.

Lick and a promise. Doing something quickly but promising to be more thorough next time.

Lie like a pig in shit. To tell lies with great skill.

Lily. An effeminate man.

Lipstick on the dipstick. Apocryphal evidence that fellatio has been performed.

Liquid amber. Beer. Also liquid lunch.

Liquid laugh. Vomit.

Little man in the boat. The clitoris.

Little rain hat. A condom. ⚲

Little woman. The wife. (♀)

Little white mice. Tampons. 'The little white mice are in today'.

Load. A venereal infection.

Log. A lazy, virtually immobile person.

Lolly water. Any drink other than beer.

Loo. A toilet.

Looker. An attractive woman. (♀)

Loop. A fool.

Lord Muck. A pretentious social-climbing man.

Lounge lizard. A heterosexual man (♂) who takes an untoward interest in socialising with women.

Love handles. Cellulite, spare tyres, beer gut.

Love bite. A deliberate bruise on the neck or body, ostensibly given in the height of passion but more frequently a symbol of triumph or territoriality.

Love juice. Sexual secretions.

Love muscle. The penis.

Love nest. An illicit venue for Funny Business.

Lovers' balls. A mild case of orchitis, (∞) supposedly brought on by prolonged sexual activity or by lack of same: 'Too much thoughtie, not enough naughtie'.

Low wheel. A prostitute. (♀)

Lubra. Aboriginal woman. ♀ res

Lubra's loincloth. Unit of measurement of uncleanliness (cf Abo's armpit).

Lummox. A fat stupid person.

Lubricated. Drunk.

Lucky legs. Legs so thin their owner is lucky they don't snap off and go right up the bum.

Lunatic soup. Any strong alcoholic drink, chiefly brandy or rum.

Maiden's water

M

Mad. Insane.
(1) Mad as a cut snake.
(2) Mad as a a meat axe.
(3) Mad as a two-bob watch.

Maddie. A masturbatory exercise; to have a maddie. *μλκ*

Madhaddock. A crazy person.

Mad rooter. Any woman who expresses interest or enthusiasm during intercourse. *(♀)*

Madwoman. A woman whose behaviour is anti-social, hence "All over the place like a madwoman's breakfast/piss". *(♀)*

Maggot. A useful term of abuse, implying an insignificant being who lives in filth.

Magic word. Fuck. A person using this person inappropriately is said to 'have dropped the magic word'. *φ*

Maiden's water. Weak tea.

Make. To have sexual relations: Make it, make love, make jig-a-jig.

Mallee root. Prostitute. Rhyming slang.

Mangy. Extremely unkempt, scabby, decrepit.

Mantrap. An unduly attractive woman who aims to use her wiles to acquire wealth, status or marriage and is almost impossible to resist.

Map of Tasmania. The female pudendum.

Marble orchard. A cemetery.

Marbles. Testicles.

Mary. A female aborigine; also an offensive form of address for an effeminate man.

Mary Pickford in three acts. Washing only the face, hands and those bits. (See French bath).

Match. 'Your face and my bum'. Primary school side-splitter.

Matinee. Afternoon sexual intercourse.

Meat. Genitalia. 'Girl meets boy in park; boy parks meat in girl'.

Meditation room. Toilet.

Melons. Breasts.

Merchant. A specialist. e.g. panic merchant, piss merchant.

Merkin. The female pudendum. A

merkin was originally a pubic wig, worn to disguise the ravages of venereal disease.

Merkin, Jerkin' and Ferkin'. The erotic trilogy symbolising the female parts, the auto-erotic and the intimately interpersonal.

Mermaid. One of those terms of insult which improves with explanation: a mermaid is a little cunt with scales.

Merry. Moderately drunk.

Mick. A Roman Catholic.

Mickey. The female genitals.

Michael. The more formal term of address for the female genitalia than Mickey.

Middle leg. The penis.

Midge. Someone of diminished stature.

Migrant. This seemingly innocuous term for someone recently arrived in the country became a standard term of abuse in the 1950s and was officially replaced by New Australian.

Milk bar cowboy. One who makes a great show of style and bravado but is really a Wanker, Gutless wonder, Bullshit artist.

Minute man. One who can manage to ejaculate in less than 60 seconds.

Mixed company. Any social group in which women are present; the expression may be used as a warning that some men should tone down their language.

Mongrel. Someone of mixed race. During the Golden Years of Australian Racism (1788 until more recently than you might think) this was a major insult and remains an expression used more for enemies than friends.

Mokey. The female pudendum.

Monkey fuck. Lighting a cigarette from the end of one already lit.

Monthly. The menstrual period.

Mooning. A communal display of bare buttocks in order to offend the viewer. Maori dissidents in New Zealand, for whom this is an ancient and honourable means of expressing scorn, have been arrested for performing the act before Royalty.

Moo. A stupid woman. (From cow, a term more offensive in Britain than Australia).

Morning glory. Sexual intercourse upon waking up.

Mother-fucker. Expression of disgust or contempt (from US). The only real swearword to be invented in two centuries by a nation normally renowned for its creativity. Often shortened to 'mother' or, as it essentially a Black American expression, 'muthah'.

Mother's ruin. Gin.

Mountain oysters. Lamb testicles.

Mouse. Tight as a mouse's ear: A sexually inexperienced girl.

Mrs Murray. A toilet.

Mrs Palmer and her five daughters. The hand, as a masturbatory aid.

Muff. The female pudendum. Hence muff-diver for one who practises cunnilingus.

Muffin. The female pudendum. Again!

Muggins. The poor mug who ends up getting stuck with something: a bill, a job etc.

Mundrum. A variety of muff or muffin.

Mug lair. A flashy young man with loud tastes. (see Lair).

• **Mushroom.** Someone not properly informed of what is going on. A mushroom is kept in the dark and fed on bullshit.

Musical milk. Methylated spirits mixed with water.

Mutton. The penis.

My oath. Yes.

Myrtle. Sexual intercourse.

Nancy boy. A homosexual.

Nasties. The sexual parts.

Nasty. Sexual intercourse. Also, nattum.

Nature calls. A polite way of excusing oneself to attend to personal ablutions or even to take a crap.

Naughty. Sexual intercourse (cf thoughty).

Naughty bits. The genitals or the erotic sections of books or films.

Naughty forty-eight. See Dirty Weekend.

Nelly's death. Cheap wine.

New chum. Originally a new convict (chum meant inmate in prison slang) but later any immigrant.

Newstime. An element of primary school education designed to entertain teachers with every intimate detail of the parents' private life.

Niagaras. Niagara Falls: balls. RS ∞
Rhyming slang.

Niff. A bad smell.

Night cart. A sanitary truck.

Nigger. Aborigine or any other person RS
of non-Caucasian race. The Bulletin
magazine said, in 1887: 'No nigger, no
Chinaman, no Lascar, no Kanaka, no
purveyor of cheap coloured labour is
an Australian'. A legendary story is
told of the American negro entertainer
on stage with a troupe of female
impersonators. The crowd gave him a
hard time but he was saved by the
compere who said: 'All right you lot. If
you don't give the nigger a fair go I'11
bring the poofs back on'. Also a blackfish
and an obligatory name for a black dog.

Nine holer. A toilet for communal
use. One vintage example, in
Richmond NSW, has been classified as
a vital Australian historical site by
the National Trust.

• **Nine inches of heaven.**
(1) The penis (as defined by men).
(2) Two penises (as defined by women).

Nip. Japanese. Japan is pronounced RS
Nippon in Japanese. Given the
altercation between Australia and
Japan in World War II and the
unreasonable attitude taken by
Japanese industry towards our coal
unions it seems odd that Nip and Jap
are the best — and worst — we can
come up with.

Nit. A fool.

Noah. Noah's Ark — shark.

Nob. The penis. One speaks of going to the men's toilet 'where the big nobs hang out'. To spell this as Knob shows the profoundest ignorance.

Noddy. A condom.

Nookie. Sexual intercourse. Hence the amusement at passing the Shady Nook Motel.

Norks. Breasts. Believed to be from Norco butter which once featured a large udder on its wrapper. Hated by girls named Nola, Nellie, Nerida etc who invariably end up victims of alliteration.

Normanton cocktail. A gin and two blankets.

Nosebag. A condom.

Nose rag. Handkerchief.

NRNRH. No Root, No Ride Home. Popular motoring motto.

Nubbies. Breasts.

Nuddy. Naked.

Nugget. A small but perfectly formed man.

Number.
(1) A marijuana cigarette.
(2) A con trick or convoluted explanation.

Number ones. Wee wee.

Number twos. Poo poos.

Nungers. Breasts. ∞

Nurtle. Sexual intercourse. ♀

Nuts. Do one's nuts over. To be obsessively infatuated.

Nut man. A homosexual. (♂)

Nuthouse. A hospital for the mentally ill.

Nympho. Nymphomaniac. A woman who wants a man to keep kissing her after he's had an orgasm. (♀)

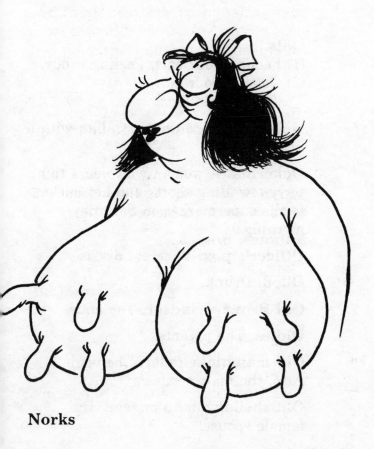

Norks

O

Oats.
(1) Feeling your oats. Feeling randy.
(2) Getting your oats.
  (Congratulations).

rcs?

Ocker. An uncouth Australian with a heart of gold.

(♀)

Ockerina. A woman who wears tight terry-towelling shorts and haircurlers to the supermarket on Saturday mornings.

Officer's pox: Venereal disease.

Oiled. Drunk.

ω

Old Brown Windsor. The anus.

Oldies. The parents.

| (♂)

Old man/bloke/feller. The penis. Also, the male spouse.

(♀)

Old sheila/woman/cheese. The female spouse.

Old man/bloke/feller

Off. Foul, disgusting or tasteless. Anything from a fart to an inappropriate remark can be considered 'off'.

Off. Rapid or swift:
- (1) Off like a bride's nightie.
- (2) Off like a robber's dog.
- (3) Off like a harlot's drawers.

On.
- (1) On the job. Involved in sexual intercourse.
- (2) On the piss. Drinking alcohol excessively.
- (3) On a sure thing. Having been told about a winning racehorse.
- (4) On the nest. In bed having sexual intercourse.

One-eared elephant. Popular party trick where a man offers to show the company a one-eared elephant. He pulls out his side trouser pocket then unzips his fly. Depending on the company this could go further but rarely does.

One-eyed trouser snake. The penis.

One-armed. Indicating frenetic activity:
- (1) Busy as a one-armed (wall) paper hanger.
- (2) Busy as a one-armed taxi-driver with crabs.

One night stand. A brief but meaningful relationship.

Onion. Group sex where only one of

the group is female.

Optic. A look at someone attractive. From rhyming slang optic nerve — perve. q.v.

< RS

Oranges. Breasts.

∞

Orchestra stalls. Balls (testicles). Rhyming slang.

∞

Ort. The anus.

ω

Oscar. A pervert.

Overnight bag. A woman available for a one-night stand.

(♀)

• **Oyster.** Trying to put an oyster in a parking meter. Sexual impotence caused by alcohol (see Brewers).

P

Pacifier. A policeman's club or nightstick.

≠ US

Packet of salts. To go through a woman like a packet of salts is to swiftly initiate sexual activity and to conclude the operation with equal speed.

φ

Pack shit. To be afraid. Also pack death.

Paddy. A fit of temper.

Paddywhack. A beating or spanking.

Pakapoo ticket. Toilet roll or a pack of poo tickets. The existence of Chinese lottery 'pakapoo' tickets is sometimes claimed as the origin of this phrase. We are not convinced.

Pain in the arse/neck. A tedious person or thing.

Paki. A Pakistani.

rcs

Pansy. An effeminate homosexual.

(♂)

Pants. Get into someone's pants. To have sex with.

Pantsman. A man with a higher than average sex drive.

Paperbag job. Someone so physically unattractive you have to put a paper bag over their heads before sleeping with them. Also the punchline to a long and tedious joke which we can't be bothered telling you right now.

Parachute. A fart.

Paralytic. Extremely drunk.

Pasho session. An extended bout of kissing, fondling and ear nibbling.

Passionkillers. Tight female underclothes, particularly long step-ins.

Passion pit. A cinema where pasho sessions take place. Traditionally suburban fleapits or drive-ins. The video boom has diminished their number although pashing remains at the same level.

Pasties. Gaudy nipple covers worn by strippers.

Pears. Breasts.

Pee. To urinate.

Peel. To divest onself of clothes.

Pelican shit. Unit of measurement of height. A tall person is a long streak of pelican shit.

Pelican's breakfast. A drink of water and a look around.

Percy. The penis.

Perform.
(1) To swear, to lose one's temper.
(2) To have sexual intercourse.

Perisher. A drunken spree.

Perk. To vomit.

Perve. To observe the female form from a distance while having impure thoughts. *Optic nerve*

Phallus. Popular contemporary term for the penis. Good to see that Latin *(Greek)* still has a practical use.

Philip McCavity. See Ben Doon.

Pick-up. A casual sexual acquaintance.

Piece de resistance. Constipation.

Pie eater. A small-timer.

Pigeon.
(1) To spit on someone from above.
(2) A fool, dupe, victim.

Piglet. A female adolescent who looks likely to become a Grunter.

Pig's arse/bum/ear/eye. Expressing disbelief.

Pig night. A social event where the men have a contest as to who can bring the ugliest woman to a dance or a party. A prize may or may not be awarded. Popular among football and surf clubs. It is considered bad form to give the game away to the ladies concerned.

Piker. A scaredy cat, one who refuses a difficult task at the last moment.

Pillow biter. Passive homosexual. (♂) (See Receiver).

Pimp.
(1) One who solicits for prostitutes.
(2) A tattletale.

Pinko. Drunk on methylated spirits.

Pirate. Man who habitually picks up (♂) women in public places, streets, bars.

Piss. Urine, alcohol.

Piss-easy. Very easy.

Pissing down. Raining heavily.

(Piece of) piss. Very easy.

Piss about. To fool around.

Piss away. To waste.

Pissing in someone's pocket. Being sycophantic.

Piss off. Usually a command to go away, or to make them angry.

Piss someone off. To send someone away. Or to make them angry

Piss on. To go on drinking into the morning.

Piss all over. To beat comprehensively.

● **(I wouldn't) piss on him if he were**

on fire. To hold someone in complete contempt.

Piss ant or pissant. Small person who is still able to cause annoyance.

Pissaphone. Funnel-shaped military urinal for tropical use.

Pissed. Drunk. Pissed as a parrot! Pissed to the eyeballs.

Piss elegant. Excessively stylish.

Pisspot. A drunkard.

Pissed-off. Extremely annoyed.

(o) **Pissflaps.** The labia majora. Also a term of abuse.

Piss fart. To waste time.

Pissing fish-hooks. Symptom of urinary tract infection or venereal disease. *Ιρβὰ. κατουρας ξυραράκια (τό λεγεο Άγις ο Κασάξης)*

Piss-up. A party marked by huge consumption of alcohol.

Pissy. Small, insignificant.

Piss weak. Mean and contemptuous. A poor performance.

Pit stop. A pause in a journey to refuel, usually with beer.

Plastered. Drunk.

Plat. A fool.

rCS **Plate face.** An ᴬasian. *orthographic xenophobia?*

φ×ɴ **Play around.** Sexual promiscuity.

(φ) **Play up.** To engage in sexual activity in the absence of the regular partner.

Play silly buggers. To act the fool.

Plonk. Cheap wine. A mispronunciation of blanc (white) French wine offered to troops during WWI.

Pocket billiards. Playing with the genitals via hands in the trouser pockets. More implied than actually performed. A popular expression of male authority in Australia has been to require the man of inferior status to take his hands out of his pockets and an implication of self-abuse can add weight to the instruction.

[handwritten marginal note: Πρββ. το δικο μας / το Βγάλ' τα χέρια / απ' τις τσέπες!]

Pot-walloper. A big boozer.

Plonko. An alcoholic.

Plop. Faeces.

Po. A chamber pot. *[handwritten marginal note: Πρββ. το πω/πω (< French pot)]*

Pod. In pod — pregnant. See Up the duff.

Podge. Someone chubby.

Po faced. Deadpan. A face as expressionless as a chamber pot.

Point Percy at the porcelain. To urinate.

Poke.
(1) To have intercourse.
(2) A woman as a sex object. 'She'd make a good poke'.

Poke borak. To make fun of someone.

Politician. A public figure. (See Bag Man, Poofter, Piss Off, Arsehole etc).

Pollinating. To go out on sexual expeditions. 'Where are you going tonight? Out pollinating!'

Pommy. A person of British ancestry. Arguments rage as to the origin of the word. Some people swear blind that convicts had POME, or Prisoner of Mother England, stencilled on their clothes or documents. Others suggest that their faces were as red as pomegranates when they stepped off the sailing ships. POME is a complete fabrication and the faces of people just off a four-month voyage tended to be pale or green! The answer is simple rhyming slang: immigrant — pomegranate. From which we get an abbreviated pommy. So there!

Pommy bastard. A person of British origin with no redeeming features. Tautological.

Ponce. Originally a pimp; also a weedy lair.

Poncess. A prostitute who keeps a man.

Poo. Faeces. In the poo: in any kind of trouble.

Poo shooter. A homosexual.

Pong. A Chinaman.

Ponk. A bad smell.

Poof. A homosexual. From puff, the 1870s expression for a sodomite.

Poofter (poofta). A homosexual,

usually effeminate. A derogatory term used also to heterosexuals, usually light-heartedly. Can apply to anyone connected with academia or the performing arts. Popular expression since the 1940s.

Poofter-basher. One who beats up homosexuals.

Poon. Sexual degenerate. The classic description is a dirty old man who goes out sniffing ladies' bicycle seats on hot days.

Pooper scooper. Originally the term (♂) for a utensil designed for collecting dogshit; accepted with glee as a new term for homosexuals.

POQ. Piss Off Quick. To depart rapidly.

Poopcatchers. Trousers tied at the ankle.

Poophole pal. A homosexual. (♂)

Pop a joey. To experience the miracle of childbirth.

Poppyshow. Flashing the thighs and underwear.

•**Pork.** Like a pork chop at a Jewish wedding. Ill-at-ease. Out of place.

Pork sword. The penis. Also: sink the pork sword.

Porky. Fat. Traditional Australian name for a fat dog . . .

Porno. Pornography: the gratuitous presentation of sexual material. Hmm!

Poopcatchers

Potboiler. An inferior piece of literature produced for financial gain. (C'mon now!)

Powder room. The women's toilet. The mirrors are bigger but you have to pee sitting down.

Powerpoint. Asian immigrant. So named because their eyes slope like a powerpoint. Recent Laotian, Cambodian and Vietnamese arrivals can feel proud that like the new chums, remittance men, poms, reffos, dagos and wogs before them, they now have their very own abusive title and have been welcomed into Australian society by the previous generation of immigrants.

Pox doctor One who specialises in the pox (venereal disease). Also Dressed Up like a pox doctor's clerk. Flashy and ill-dressed.

Pratfall. To slip over on your bum.

Prawn. Don't come the raw prawn. Don't try to deceive me.

Prawnhead. A general term of abuse, implying lack of intelligence and homeliness.

Prawn night. A feast of crustaceans and beer, not necessarily in that order.

Preggers. Up the duff, in the family way, a bun in the oven. Expecting a blessed event.

Pretty boy. An effeminate young man.

Prick. The penis. Also a term of abuse. We have noted elsewhere that while a man can be called a cunt, a woman is not called a prick, though there have been developments recently in some areas of comedy cabaret where nothing is impossible. Or funny.

Prick with ears. A form of abuse, redolent with imagery.

Prickteaser. A flirtatious woman who appears to promise more than she is prepared to deliver.

Promise. To be on a promise. To be assured of sexual intercourse.

Pro. A prostitute. Also a prozzo.

Proposition. To suggest a sexual liaison.

Prominent Racing Identity. SP bookmaker.

Pub crawl. A visit to a variety of hostelries with the purpose of ingesting alocholic liquor.

Pubes. Pubic hair.

Pud. The penis. A fine word dating from the time of Charles II.

Pulling the pud: Literally masturbating but can also imply timewasting. 'C'mon, get going, don't just stand there pulling your pud.'

Pudding club. An exclusive organisation for the pregnant.

Pudding face. A plump, unhealthy visage.

Puggim. Fucking (Aboriginal dialect).

Puke. To vomit.

Pull.
(1) Pull oneself off. To masturbate.
(2) Pull your finger out. Get working.
(3) Pull a sheila. To win a young
   lady's attention.
(4) Pull up. To end an activity. 'How
   did you pull up after the piss-up?'

Punce. A homosexual. Also the
female pudenda.

Punch one through. To have sexual intercourse.

Puppies. Breasts. A young woman
who loses her bikini top in the surf
and modestly covers her breasts with
her arms may be asked: 'Hey lady, if
you're going to drown those puppies
can I have the one with the brown nose?'

Pushing shit uphill. To attempt the
impossible. Frequently done, or not
done, with a pointy stick.

Pussy. The vagina.

Pussy whipped. Completely in thrall
to a woman.

Pussy pelmet. A very short
mini-skirt.

Putdown. An insult.

Put-on. Fakery.

Putty. Useless. Replaces Up To Shit
in polite company.

Put on Jam. To be pretentious
(popular expression last century).

Quandong

$(♀)$ **Quandong.** A woman who fails to come across despite being wined and dined with that end in mind.

$(♂)$ **Queen/Queer.** Homosexual (old-fashioned).

Queen up. To dress in women's clothes.

⚤ **Quickie.** Speedily completed sexual intercourse. The male traditionally tells the female: 'Just because I was quick please don't think I didn't enjoy it.'

○ **Quim.** The vagina.

$(♂)$ **Quince.** An effeminate man.

ω **Quoit.** The anus.

Race off. To seduce. Popular expression from the 1960s.

Rack off. To leave. May be issued as an instruction; a mild form of 'fuck off'.

Rags. Having the rags on. Menstruating.

Rah rah. A man who plays Rugby Union football and engages in the largely alcoholic and oafish social life connected with the sport.

Raining.
(1) If it was raining pea soup I'd be holding a fork.
(2) If it was raining virgins I'd be in jail with a poofter.

Randy. Erotically aroused, generally with no particular place to go.

Rare as rocking horse shit. Extremely rare.

Raspberry. A farting noise made

with the lips. (From rhyming slang: raspberry tart — fart).

Rat. I'd be up her like a rat up a drainpipe. Very quickly if given the chance.

Ratbag. General term of abuse for a stupid or deluded person. An eccentric, particularly a very persistent one.

Rathouse. A lunatic asylum.

Ratshit. Woeful, disastrous. The night was ratshit.

Raw. Naked. 'In the raw': popular alternative chorus to the song Running Bear.

Razz. To tease, to give someone the razz, to razz them (From raspberry).

Reading room. The toilet. Australasian Post, Woman's Day and Phantom comics are a vital ingredient.

Receiver. Passive homosexual who plays the feminine role. (See Pillow). We are still waiting to hear from our American football correspondent on the role of the Wide Receiver.

Red flag. Menstruation.

Red ned. Cheap red wine. Also tomato sauce.

Reffo. Refugee. Any European emigrating to Australia after World War II. Notorious for polluting good plain Aussie food with garlic, replacing good plain Aussie football codes with soccer and painting their good plain Aussie houses pink and blue and other poofter colours.

RFM. A Rat Faced Moll. A not particularly attractive woman. (♀)

Reginalds. Underwear. (Rhyming slang: Reg Grundys — undies). <RS

Rocking horse shit. Unit of measurement of rarity or scarcity.

Richard. Had the Richard — polite form of had the dick. The male organ is NOT a Richard, nor is it appropriate to call someone a Richardhead.

Ride. Sexual intercourse. Also a woman available for same. φ (♀)

Rider of the chocolate canyon. A homosexual. (♂)

Ring. The anus. ω

Ripped. Stoned or drunk. Popularly expressed as 'ripped to the tits'. (Male or female).

Rise in the world. To get a kick in the bum.

Roadapple. Horse manure. (⬭)

Rock-ape. A neo-simian person.

Rockchopper. A Roman Catholic. ᴠᴄs The suggestion that the word refers to Catholic convicts breaking rocks overestimates the creativity. The nickname is simply formed from the letters R and C.

Rod. The penis. ᴵ

Roger. The penis.

Roger the lodger. Someone present in a house and suspected of sexual motives. A derogatory term.

Root. The act of sexual intercourse.

(Wouldn't you) Root your boot: Goodness me.

Rooted. Worn-out, exhausted.

Ropeable. Extremely angry.

Rort.
(1) A con game or dubious scheme. 'The whole land deal was a rort.'
(2) A wild party. 'Shit, last night was a rort.' Rotten. Drunk.

Rough. Promiscuous, sleazy, vulgar.

Rough as guts. Also rough as bags. Sleazy, vulgar.

Rough moll. An uncouth young lady who invariably travels in public with one or more friends of similar demeanour.

Rugger bugger. One who plays Rugby Union football, attends private school and shares communal showers after the match.

Rumble seat. The backside.

Runs.
(1) Diarrhoea.
(2) Getting runs on the board (a cricketing metaphor): having success in sexual activity.

Saigon Rose. A supposedly incurable form of syphilis rampant in wartime Vietnam. Some see it as a fictional and ineffective invention to enourage soldiers to take more precautions.

AC

Sambo. A member of the African race.

rcs

San-man. Nightsoil collector, dunny man. Reputed to drive the fastest truck in Australia because it has 60 pisstins.

(♂)

Sauce. Liquor. Also sauced: drunk.

Sausage. The penis. (See Sink).

|

Scab. A strikebreaker, one who works when union members are on strike.

(♂⚥)

Scabby. Of an unattractive and unpleasant appearance.

Score. To succeed in obtaining casual sexual intercourse.

φ

Screw. To have sexual intercourse.

φ

Scrubber. A rough girl with loose morals. Usually unkempt. (♀)

Scumbag. Low despicable person.

Scunge. A dirty person. Also scungy: messy, unkempt.

Seatman. An aggressive homosexual. (♂)

Secco. A sex maniac.

Secondhand Sue. An old, unattractive prostitute or homosexual. (♀ ♂)

See a man about a dog. To leave without giving a reason, usually to urinate.

Septic. Septic tank. A Yank. Rhyming slang. RS >

Sexed up. Tumescent (women only). It was traditionally supposed that women needed to be sexed up rather than attain that state unaided.

Sexpot. A blatantly sexual woman. Usually very attractive and provocatively dressed. Usually with somebody else. (♀)

Sweet fuck all. Next to nothing.

Shag. To perform sexual intercourse. Also Shagged: Worn-out (cf rooted). ♀

Shagger. Cheerful nickname used in greeting. Does not imply that the addressee is a notorious cocksman, more often a general expression of heterosexual bonhomie.

Shagger's back. Any pain in the back, usually boasted of as being due to intercourse.

Shaggin' waggon. A panel van with mattress in the back. (See Fuck Truck).

Shake hands with the wife's best friend. To urinate.

Shake the dew off the lily. Removing the last drops from the urethra after urination. Hence also the expression 'I'll be with you in two shakes'. (If it takes more than two shakes see a urologist).

Shark. Lower than shark shit. Despicable.

Shat. Past tense of shit. *Here we get some grammar.*

Shiney Bob. Someone with a high opinion of himself.

Sheep dip. Cheap rough booze.

Sheila. The all-enduring Australian reference to a woman. Originally Irish, opposite of Paddy, though bloke has become the general Australian word for a male. ♀

Shickered. Drunk. Popular expression adopted from the Yiddish. *< Yiddish ?*

Shinybum. Any desk worker.

Shim. A transsexual (a she/him). ☿

Shirt-lifter. A male homosexual. *(♂)*

Shit. Excrement.
(1) Have or get the shits. To be annoyed.
(2) Give someone the shits. To annoy

someone.

(3) Shit hit the fan. There was trouble.

(4) In the shit. In trouble.

(5) Not worth a pinch of shit. Worthless.

(6) Put shit on. To run down or criticise.

(7) To shit in. To win comfortably.

Shitcan. To denigrate or ridicule.

Shitfaced. Extremely drunk.

Shit-for-brains. Stupid. The phrase must always be used with its hyphens.

Shithead. A worthless person either mean or stupid.

Shit hot. Excellent, first class.

Shithouse. A lavatory. Terrible (cf ratshit).

Shitkicker. A lowly paid employee doing menial work.

Shitless. Absolutely, as in scared shitless.

Shit on the liver. To be in a bad temper. Also crack a shitty.

Shits or running shits. Diarrhoea.

Shit-stirrer. A trouble-maker, usually in union/political matters.

Shitty. Several degrees less than delighted.

Shoot one's bolt. To ejaculate.

Short and curlies. Pubic hairs.

Short arm. The penis.

Short arse. A short person. Also: short stuff.

Shot. Drunk.

Shouse. Shithouse; either a privy or an overall miserable, unwell feeling.

Shout. To buy a round of drinks.

Shrimp. A short person (in USA, a barbecued crustacean).

Sickie. An unofficial day off work. 'I'm going to ring in and take a sickie so I can go to the beach'.

Shypoo. Cheap grog.

Sillybuggers. A mythical game supposedly played by a person trying to avoid work or be deceptive. 'What do you think you're doing, playing sillybuggers?'

Silly syrup. Alcohol. Also singing syrup.

Sin Bin.
(1) See Shaggin' Wagon and Fuck Truck.
(2) A penalty area at sporting matches. Unlike the original the players have already sinned before they're there.

Sink the sausage. Sexual intercourse. Also sink the sav (saveloy).

Sissy. An effeminate boy or man.

Sixty-niner. The position for mutual oral sex. Oral sex is so named because it is something Australians talk about but rarely do.

Skidmark. The visible traces of excrement on one's underwear.

Skinny dipping. Nude swimming.

♀ **Skirt.** A woman. A nice bit of skirt.

Skive. To avoid work, to skive off.

Skun. To drink all someone's liquor. Sometimes done by crashing a party with an empty wine bottle, behaving so as to be thrown out and leaving in high dudgeon with the nearest full bottle.

(♀) **Slag.** A woman of notorious moral laxity.

rcs **Slanteye.** An Asian. Also, Slope (see Powerpoint).

Slash. To urinate. 'I'm going outside for a slash'.

(o) **Slats.** The labia. Threatening to kick a man in the slats implies a threat to his masculinity.

Sleazo. An unpleasant lowlife person.

Slewed. Drunk. Also Sloshed.

Slip a joey. To have a miscarriage.

Slug. A slow, slimy person.

(♀) **Slut.** An unkempt, slatternly, promiscuous woman.

(♀) **Slutguts.** Term of address for a slut.

Slops. Beer.

Sloppy seconds. In group sex, the term for those who follow the leader.

Smart arse. Know-all.

Smashed. Drunk or stoned.

Smelly. A fart.

Smoo. Sexual fluid or secretions.

Smooge. To flatter or romance someone.

Snail trail. A woman. Used as an expression of disgust by homosexuals.

Snakes. Going for a Snakes' (Hiss: Piss). Rhyming slang.

Snake's belly. Lower than a snake's belly. Despicable.

Snatch. The vagina. Originally meant hasty copulation.

Snowdropper. Pervert who steals women's underwear from clothesline.

Snoozer. A baby.

Snork. A baby.

Snow bunny. Woman available for apres-ski activities.

Soak. A drunkard.

S.O.B. Son of a Bitch. This expression is thought so shocking by Americans that they use the abbreviation, a source of confusion for many Australians who assume it stands for Silly Old Bugger or Stupid Old Bastard and are disappointed to discover it is actually a very mild epithet by our standards.

Sod. An unpleasant person who may

be told to sod (bugger) off.

Sort. An attractive sheila; a good sort.

Souse. A drunkard.

Southerner. In Queensland a Southerner is a communist sex pervert who wants you to pay too much tax. In North Queensland this term includes people from Brisbane.

Sozzled. Drunk.

Spag. An Italian.

Spaghetti eater. Obsolete term of abuse for an Italian, from the days when the consumption of such exotic delicacies was considered highly suspect.

Spazzo. Spastic. Not necessarily a handicapped person, a spazzo can be anyone weak or unco-ordinated.

Spifflicate. Bash, assault. An old Irish term brought here last century by that tiny minority of Irishmen who like to drink and brawl.

Sportsmen's gap. The vagina.

Sparrow fart. Early morning, dawn. 'I'll meet you at sparrow fart'.

Spoggie. A condom.

Spit. The big spit. Vomit (see Yawn).

Spit out the dummy. To give up something pleasant for the sake of temporarily expressing rage.

Splash the boots. To urinate.

Splash the boots

Spoof. Semen.

Spunk.
(1) Semen
(2) A young, sexually attractive
    person.

Spunk rat. A very attractive young
person indeed.

Spurge. An effeminate man. (♂)

Squarehead. A German. rcs

Squiff. A drunkard. He is squiffy.

Stacked. Big-breasted. ♀

Stag. An erection.

Starkers. Naked . . . stark-naked.

Steam. Methylated spirits, as a beverage. Also, sting.

Steeltits. An authoritative woman (See Iron maiden).

Stiff. An erect penis.

Stiffy. Another erect penis; use of this expression implies that it is held in great respect by its owner.

Stick it up your arse. 'I don't want it thank you'.

Stinko. Drunk. Also, stonkered.

Stinkfinger. Playing stinkfinger. Putting a finger in the vagina. A derogatory expression used by a young man's friends who have probably not been performing that particular act.

Stirrer. Radical extremist, troublemaker. Anyone with deeply held convictions.

Stoush. A brawl.

Street Arab. Teenage gang member, juvenile delinquent.

Stuff. To have sexual intercourse (cf root, shag, fuck).

Stuffed. Worn-out exhausted.

Get stuffed (A polite form of get fucked). Not an invitation to sex but a fine, all-purpose curse in the classic sense of wishing a person confused, confounded and damned.

Stuffed-up. Bungled.

Stung. Drunk. Also, stunned.

Suck.
(1) Suck it and see. An invitation to test something out.
(2) Suck off. Orgasm by oral stimulation.
(3) Suck-holer. Sycophant.

Sugar daddy. Worldwide expression (♂) for an older man who spends money on a younger woman and expects a return on his investment.

Sun. He thinks the sun shines out of his arse. To have an inordinately high opinion of oneself.

Sunnies. Breasts.

Superdupers. Large breasts.

Sweet. She's sweet. Meaning everything is all right.

Sweet fuck all. Very little (cf SFA).

Swinger. Someone who exchanges sexual partners. (See Wife swapping).

Swippington. Drunk.

Swish. The sound made by a homosexual entering a room.

Switch hitter. Bi-sexual.

Sword. Penis, hence:
(1) Sink the pork sword (intercourse)
(2) Cross swords. Men standing side by side at a urinal.

Tabby. A girl. (♀)

ω

Tail. The gluteus maximus or bum.

Take the piss. To mock imitate, satirise or deflate. 'We really took the piss out of Jonno'.

Talent. Potential sexual partners at a social occasion. 'To check out the talent'.

(♂) **Tallyman.** A de facto husband.

Tanked. Drunk.

Tan tracker. An aggressive homosexual.

▶ RS > **Tap dancer.** Cancer. (rhyming slang.)

(♀) **Tart.** A cheap woman or prostitute. Also a popular gay expression: 'Hello, Brucie, you old tart'.

Tartplate. Pillion seat on a motorcycle.

| **Tassel.** The penis.

Tatts. Tattoos. A popular form of self-

mutilation, especially in penal or
military institutions.

Team cream. Group sex in which a
number of men have sex with one girl
(cf gang bang, train).

Tear-arse. A wild, impetuous person.

Tear off a piece. To have sexual intercourse. ♂

Teaser. A more decorous form of
prickteaser. (♀)

Technicolour yawn. Vomiting.

Ten quidder. An immigrant from rcs
Britain who arrived on the assisted
passage scheme. Many returned home
(See Whingeing Poms).

Territory confetti. The pull rings
from cans of beer.

Thickhead. Fool, obtuse person.

Thirty four and a half. One half of a
sixty niner. 'You do this to me and I'll
owe you one.'

Thick. Stupid.
(1) Thick as two short planks.
(2) Thick as two Poms. rcs
(3) Thick as a brick.
(4) Thick as a log of wood.

Thing. The penis. Also, thingo or thingie. |

Third leg. Again, the penis. (

• **Thirsty enough to suck the sweat
out of a Mongolian wrestler's
jockstrap through a cane chair.**
Quite thirsty.

Thoughtie. Obscene or erotic thoughts, from think-naughty. If sex is refused, one can always say: 'If I can't have a naughty, I'll have a thoughtie'.

Three axe handles. Unit of measurement applied to the posterior of a large woman.

Throne. The lavatory bowl. Hence throne room, the loo.

Throttling pit. Communal male toilet or urinal.

Throw. To vomit. Also, to throw a map.

Thunderbox. The lavatory.

Tiddly. Drunk. From rhyming slang: tiddlywinks — drinks.

Tightarse. A miserly person. Also a virgin (female).

Tin arse. A lucky character. Also, tin bum

Tinkle, to urinate.

Tired and emotional. Journalese for pissed. 'Sir Egbert was tired and emotional last night'.

Titfer. A hat. (rhyming slang: tit for tat — hat).

Tits. Breasts.

Titting up. Stimulation of breasts and nipples: a vital element of sexual foreplay.

Toady. A flatterer, crawler, hanger-on.

Toe jam. Accumulation of grime between the toes.

Tom tits. The shits (rhyming slang). < RS

Tool. Popular euphemism for the male organ. /

Toot. Toilet.

Tossle. The male organ. !

Tosspot. A drunkard.

Touch of the tarbrush. Part negroid or Aboriginal ancestry. rcs

Tough shit. Bad luck. Also, tough titty.

Town bike. A woman who will have sex casually with any man. (Anyone can ride her). (♀)

Tonk. A fool.

Tracy bits. Tits (1920s slang). < RS ∞

Train. Pack rape. A group of men decide 'to pull the train'.

Trampoline for dick heads. A contraceptive diaphram.

Trey bits. The shits (rhyming slang). < RS Can be reduced to the treys. A trey bit, sometimes mis-spelt tray, was a threepenny coin.

Trick. A prostitute's customer.

Trog. A low form of human being.

Troppo. Mad, crazy. 'He's gone troppo'. (tropical).

Trots. Diarrhoea. Used more as a

description of the ailment itself rather than a metaphor for grumpiness. An angry person has the shits; an unwell person has the trots.

RS **Trouble and strife.** The wife.

Trouser snake. The penis. (See One-Eyed).

Trout. An unattractive dowager.

μαk **Tug.** To masturbate.

Tug

Tumble. Casual sexual intercourse.

Turd. A piece of excrement.

Turd burglar. An aggressive male homosexual.

Turd strangler. A plumber.

Turn it on. To be sexually accommodating.

Turps. Turpentine. Hence on the turps: drinking excessively.

Twang. Opium.

Twat. The vagina.

Twerp. A weedy, little person.

Twinkle. To urinate. A moderate expression fit for mixed company.

Twit. A vague, disoriented, stupid person.

Two bob. An apocryphal fee offered by homosexuals and dropped on the ground to tempt a potential Bum Chum to bend over.

Two pot screamer. A cheap drunk.

Two possums fighting in a sugar bag. Description of gyrating buttocks of attractive woman walking along in tight clothes.

Two-wheeler. A woman (rhyming slang: two-wheeler — sheila).

U

Ugly. A generic term for unattractive people. 'The uglies are out in force tonight'.

Uncle. Popular euphemism for the lover of a woman who has school-age children and does not wish to be totally embarrassed when they speak at Newstime in class.

rcs **Unbleached Australians.** Aborigines.

Underdaks. Male nether garments.

cf. par devant
,, derrière

Under the sheets. Popular game among adolescents of years gone by. One reads aloud the song titles from a Top 40 chart following each title with the words 'under the sheets'. Hence My Boyfriend's Back ... under the sheets! Always accompanied by much smirking.

Under the weather. Drunk. Common Australian expression from the 1850s.

ω/λ

Unload. To break wind.

Up. Sexual intercourse. To get up someone. Hence 'Up her like a rat up a drainpipe/a lizard up a log.'

(1) Up yours. Get stuffed
(2) Up oneself. To have an exalted high opinion of oneself.
(4) Up each other. Mutual sycophancy.
(5) Up the shit/creek. In trouble.
(6) Up the duff//spout/stick. Pregnant.
(7) Up the river. In jail.
(8) Up you for the rent/up your arse. Expression of disgust.

Up oneself

V

Vandyke. An outdoor toilet.

Valley of decision. The vagina.

Vaseline valley. A suburb or area of a town popular with homosexuals.

Vasso. Vaseline, assumed to be the major lubricant for sexual, primarily homosexual, activity. Someone jokingly accused of homosexual intentions may be asked to 'pass the vasso'.

Vatican roulette. The rhythm method of contraception or, more exactly, attempting to avoid pregnancy by refraining from intercourse at certain parts of the menstrual cycle.

Vegemite. A dark brown vegetable extract. Hence the expression drilling for Vegemite (describing an active male homosexual).

Vegie. A dull person. From vegetable.

Verbal diarrhoea. Absolute non-stop nonsense. 'He's talking shit'.

Vicar's friend. A condom.

Vino. Wine. Can be used as a general term like grog, turps, booze.

Vital statistics. The dimensions of the human form reduced to essential figures: three for women, one for men.

Vomit-making. Not all that nice.

Vital statistics

W

Wack. A weirdo.

Wacker. A crazy, eccentric person.

(†) **Wallie.** Sexual congress achieved whilst leaning against a wall.

res **Wanda.** A white man (Aboriginal word, not as offensive as Gubbo).

μɔια **Wank.** To masturbate. Also self-indulgent behaviour: Wearing nine gold chains and driving a Ferrari is a wank.

μɔκ **Wanker.** A super-egotist.

Wanking onself. To live in a dream world.

Warby. Dirty, uncouth. Old English word for maggot.

Wart. An offensive but dull person. General term of insult.

Waterbag. A teetotaller.

Water the horse. To urinate.

Waterworks. Crying.

Weaker sex. A woman. ♀

Weakie. Someone who is utterly wet and a weed.

Wee wee. To urinate. Probably in a potty, toily or on daddy's good trousers.

Wellington. Rhyming slang. <RS ⌀ Wellington boot: root. Sexual intercourse.

Werris. A Greek (rhyming slang from <RS rcs Werris Creek).

Westie. Term of scorn (Sydney) for (rcs) anyone not living within sight of a surfing beach.

Wet. Stupid, naive.

Wet arse and no fish. Description upon returning from a fruitless mission.

Wet the baby's head. An alcoholic celebration of childbirth.

Wet weekend. Menstruation.

Weirdo. Any nonconformist.

Weed. Marijuana. Also a skinny weak person.

Well endowed. Having substantial sexual appendages.

Well hung. Well-endowed but subject to the laws of gravity.

Whacko. An expression of delight. Also: Whacko the Chook, Whacko the Diddle-O.

Whack off. To masturbate.

Wham bam, thank you mam. The act of short-lived sexual intercourse.

Wheat belt. A prostitute.

What are you? Rhetorical expression of the belief that the person asked the question is not very much at all.

Whingeing Pom. A derogatory term for English migrants who criticise the Lucky Country.

Whipping the dripping. Masturbation.

White-ant. To undermine or subvert. From the damage white ants do to the foundations of wooden houses.

Whopcacker. Something notably good.

Whopper. Anything unusually large.

Whore's bath. A quick rinse of the genitals.

Wife beater. A long bread loaf.

Who's up who and who's paying the rent? A complicated query into the various relationships of a number of parties i.e. politicians/police/judiciary/business.

Wick. Penis. Hence to dip the wick: sexual intercourse.

Wife swapping. Interchange of sexual partners bv mutual consent for temporary adventure.

Wife's best friend. The penis.

Willie. The penis.

Wimp. A moral and physical coward and weakling.

Winedot. An alcoholic. Also, wino.

Wobbly. A fit or a tantrum.

Wog. A foreigner, usually middle-eastern. The popular derivation is Wily Oriental Gentleman. Used for any Southern European in Australia. (See Reffo). *rcs*

Wog. To spit.

Wogball. Soccer.

Wombat. A man who uses a woman for sex and free meals without showing respect or affection. A wombat is an animal that eats, roots and leaves.

Wool. Pubic hair.

Wop. Southern European. *rcs*

Working girl. A prostitute. *(♀)*

Wrong 'un. A crook, a devious person.

Water the horse

Yawn

Yahoo. An oaf or a yobbo.

res

Yamidgee. An Aborigine.

Yawn. Vomit. Also technicolour yawn.

res (♀)

Yellow satin. A Chinese woman.

res

Yid. Jewish person (from the Yiddish language spoke by Central European jews).

Yike. A brawl or a stoush.

/i ⌐u

Yob. An oaf, larrikin, street tough. Affectionate dimunitive is yobbo. See what you get when you spell yob backwards? Clever, huh?

• **Yodel up the valley.** Cunnilingus.

Zipper sniffer

Zipper sniffer. A cruising male homosexual.

Zit. A pimple. (US origin).

Zonked. Advanced state of semi-consciousness caused by excessive ingestion of alcohol or drugs.

Zubrick. The penis.

Folk etymology:

beresk (< berserk) 'bereft ; upset'